"*In an era of proposals involving quick turnarounds of educational delivery systems, the authors have shared a long-term high stakes process for rethinking how schools do business while maintaining a focus on both Real World Learning and Following the Child. This has the potential to change the landscape of public education nationwide.*"

—Dan Lawson, Superintendent of Schools
Tullahoma City Schools, TN

"Off the Clock *generates urgency for school systems to begin focusing on the whole child's education. The New Hampshire model sets the stage for schools to implement their theories of action so student achievement can increase system-wide.*"

—Elizabeth Alvarez, Principal
Chicago Public School, IL

"*An impressive account of New Hampshire's journey from time-based teaching to competency-based learning,* Off the Clock *presents the rationale, process, challenges, and key learnings from that state's quest for zero dropouts and substantive, sustainable secondary school redesign. Based on firsthand involvement in the inception and implementation of the change process,* Off the Clock *is as informative as it is inspirational.*"

—Kim Carter, Executive Director
QED Foundation

"*The authors identify important issues about learning, show what they did to invoke changes, and provide alternatives that can be used in schools, districts, and states. This book challenges educators to create alternative means for students to meet or exceed proficiency for standards and courses.*"

—Glen Ishiwata, Former Superintendent
Moreland School District
San Jose, CA

"Off the Clock *is a delight! Bramante and Colby have given us a deeply personal, vibrant, and visionary insight into the why, what, and how of moving past the schools of old. With their hands-on knowledge, the authors take you deep into the details of New Hampshire's bold move from the strangling hold of the time-based Carnegie unit to a mastery-based education system. For anyone interested in competency-based learning,* Off the Clock *is a must read.*"

—Chris Sturgis, Founder
MetisNet

"*This book is an excellent resource for practitioners and leaders at the local, regional, state, and national levels. The authors offer innovative insights for restoring meaning to learning.*"

—Lyne Ssebikindu, Assistant Principal
Crump Elementary School
Memphis, TN

"*The authors have eloquently described the beginning of 21st Century Education. The move from time as the constant and high level learning as the variable to a system in which high-level learning is the constant will better equip the next generation of citizens for their futures.*"

—Jeff Herzberg, Chief Administrator
Prairie Lakes Area Education Agency
Pocahontas, IA

"*A must read on education reform in the 21st century. This book offers a how-to perspective that we can all learn from.*"

—Ann Dargon, Superintendent of Schools
Ashland Public Schools, MA

"*No more 'one size fits all.' The conversation following the must-read* Off the Clock *will transform educational models and policy into individualized learning with the essential measures of competency and accountability for student growth.*"

—Marsha M. Myles, President and CEO
Ed Tech Specialists

Off the
CLOCK

Moving Education From **TIME** to **COMPETENCY**

FRED BRAMANTE | ROSE COLBY

CORWIN
A SAGE Company

CORWIN
A SAGE Company

FOR INFORMATION:

Corwin

A SAGE Company

2455 Teller Road

Thousand Oaks, California 91320

(800) 233-9936

www.corwin.com

SAGE Publications Ltd.

1 Oliver's Yard

55 City Road

London EC1Y 1SP

United Kingdom

SAGE Publications India Pvt. Ltd.

B 1/I 1 Mohan Cooperative Industrial Area

Mathura Road, New Delhi 110 044

India

SAGE Publications Asia-Pacific Pte. Ltd.

3 Church Street

#10-04 Samsung Hub

Singapore 049483

Acquisitions Editor: Dan Alpert

Associate Editor: Megan Bedell

Editorial Assistant: Sarah Bartlett

Project Editor: Veronica Stapleton

Copy Editor: Kim Husband

Typesetter: C&M Digitals (P) Ltd.

Proofreader: Dennis W. Webb

Indexer: Sheila Bodell

Cover Designer: Michael Dubowe

Permissions Editor: Karen Ehrmann

Copyright © 2012 by Corwin

Printed in the United States of America

Library of Congress Cataloging-in-Publication Data

A catalog record of this book is available from the Library of Congress.

978-1-4522-1731-4

This book is printed on acid-free paper.

12 13 14 15 16 10 9 8 7 6 5 4 3 2 1

Contents

Acknowledgments

FRED BRAMANTE

I want to acknowledge that, without the following people, I would not have been in a position to write this book.

First, my former teachers: Ann Pratt (5th grade), who exuded the kindness that I've tried to emulate; the engaging teaching style of Brother Kevin Robert, one of the good things that I got out of high school; and Dr. Malcolm Keddy (Keene State College), who taught me to write.

I want to thank Tess Manforte for hiring me, despite my GPA, and Ron Domonkos, Frank Greco, and Donald Wentworth, my mentors at Dolan Middle School, who believed that I could become a good teacher.

I want to thank former New Hampshire Governor Judd Gregg for first appointing me to the State Board of Education; Governor Craig Benson, who had enough faith in me to entrust me with the responsibility of chairing the state board and leading the redesign effort; Governor John Lynch, who allowed me to continue my work on the State Board of Education. And I want to thank former Arkansas Governor Mike Huckabee for believing in my work and allowing me to be his education advisor (2008 presidential campaign).

New Hampshire's education leaders in redesign including Dr. Leo Corriveau, my mentor and confidant, who talked me into pursuing my master's degree; Nick Donohue, who has carried forward the work that we began at the NH DOE to the Nellie Mae Education Foundation; Kim Carter, who makes this concept happen on a daily basis. To Tom Brennan, Steve Beals, Marie Ross, Gary Hunter, Chuck Ott, Dick Ayers, Bob Bickford, Skip Hanson, Steve Kosikoski; former Department of Education personnel, including Bill Ewert, Joyce Johnson, Paul Ezen, Sue McKevitt, Lorraine Patusky; and Dr. Lyonel Tracy for pulling the chestnuts out of the fire at JLCAR.

To Dr. Bob McLaughlin and the Summiteers, including Irv Richardson, Rob Fried, Mary Heath, Audrey Rogers, Laura Thomas, Mary Ford, Denise

Littlefield, John Shea, Maria Vasquez, Kim Carter, Judy Fillion, and Cathy Higgins for jump-starting the reform of educator preparation programs.

To the New Hampshire Excellence in Education Awards (EDies) steering committee, who work to recognize redesign exemplars in our state.

To Commissioner Virginia Barry and Deputy Commissioner Paul Leather for providing daily leadership in moving redesign forward on a state level and showing America that, once again, New Hampshire is First in the Nation. To my current and former State Board of Education colleagues, especially, Ray D'Amante and Deb Hamil, Daphne Kenyon, Judy Thayer, Tom Raffio, Mary McNeil, John Lyons, Bill Walker. To my interns: Chris Weeks, Jamie Richardson, Adam Letizio, and Ashley Johnson.

To Promethean Corporation for their faith in me and for their support of New Hampshire's efforts.

To Ron Fielder, Dick Hanzelka, Jason Glass, John Carver, and the rest of team Iowa's redesign leadership. To Wisconsin's CESA #1: Tim Gavigan, Keith Mardy, and Bruce Connelly. To Dr. Tom Carroll, Chris Sturgis, Susan Patrick, and Ray McNulty. Also to Jeff Herzberg, Mary Ellen Freely, and Joe DiMartino.

To Diane Schulman Davidow for contributing to the title of this book.

And to Corwin press, especially Dan Alpert and Mike Soule.

ROSE COLBY

From 2005 through 2008, high school leaders and educators struggled to understand the implications of the state rule that required students to demonstrate mastery of course competencies in order to earn credit for a course. The Capital Area Center for Educational Support (C.A.C.E.S.), one of six regional professional education centers in New Hampshire, under the leadership of Dr. Kenneth Greenbaum, developed a collaborative approach with a number of school districts to share in the work and understanding of competency development. Dr. Charles Gaides provided guidance to the project and direction to many educators as they worked toward developing high-quality competencies.

As an outgrowth of the competency development, schools soon realized that their traditional reporting out of student achievement was not compatible with competency-based learning. Rob Lukasiak, an education consultant and former math educator, was instrumental in transforming thinking from traditional mindsets in teaching and learning to documenting student mastery of learning. Much of the framework for developing competency-based assessment and grading systems evolved in working with Rob Lukasiak.

Paul Leather, Deputy Commissioner of the New Hampshire Department of Education, and Mariane Gfroerer of the New Hampshire Department of

Education provided guidance and oversight to the work of competency development at C.A.C.E.S. and within the state. The 3-year project Supporting Student Success Through Extended Learning Opportunities was a partnership between PlusTimeNH, a former nonprofit organization, the Nellie Mae Education Foundation, Q.E.D. Foundation, and the New Hampshire Department of Education. In developing the competency and grading models, many fine leaders and teachers informed this developmental work. Kim Carter of Q.E.D. expanded my experience and thinking in experiential learning. It is with gratitude and appreciation that I recognize the role of the following school leaders and educators in shaping the work in competency-based learning: Nan Parsons, Principal of Lebanon High School; Michael O'Malley, principal of Newfound High School, James LeBaron, School Redesign Coordinator at Newfound High School, and Beth Colby, Extended Learning Opportunity Coordinator; Christine Martin, currently a principal in Manchester; Steve Beals, principal of Laconia High School, Tina Green, 21st Century Learning Program Director, Laconia School District, and Lauren Streifer, Laconia High School Curriculum Coordinator; Mary Moriarty, Assistant Superintendent of Rochester Schools; Kate Zacharias, former Assistant Principal of Spaulding High School; Barbara Munsey, Superintendent of the Epping School District, Lyn Ward-Healy, Director of Professional Learning, Epping School District; Dr. Brian Blake, Superintendent of Sanborn Regional School District, Ellen Hume-Howard, Curriculum Director of Sanborn Regional School District, Brian Stack, Principal of Sanborn Regional High School, and the team of school leaders in the Sanborn School District and Gary Hunter, Manchester Extended Learning Opportunity Coordinator.

PUBLISHER'S ACKNOWLEDGMENTS

Corwin wishes to acknowledge the following peer reviewers for their editorial insight and guidance.

Elizabeth Alvarez, Principal
John C. Dore Elementary, Chicago, IL

Jay Bonstingl, Educational Consultant
Columbia, MD

Ann Dargon, Superintendent of Schools
Ashland Public Schools, Ashland, MA

Ron Fielder, Professor of Education Policy and Leadership Studies
University of Iowa

Kevin Fitzgerald, Superintendent
Caesar Rodney School District, Wyoming, DE

Jeff Herzberg, Chief Administrator
Prairie Lakes Area Education Agency, IA

Glen Ishiwata, Retired Superintendent
San Jose, CA

Dan Lawson, Director of Schools
Tullahoma City Schools, Tullahoma, TN

Marsha Myles, President
Ed Tech Specialists, MI

Tanna Nicely, Assistant Principal
Dogwood Elementary, Knoxville, TN

John R. Nori, Director of Program Development
National Association of Secondary School Principals, Reston, VA

Peggy Seigel, Education Free Agent
Education free agent LLC, Washington, DC

Lyne Ssebikindu, Elementary Principal
Crump Elementary School, Memphis, TN

Leslie Standerfer, Principal
Estrella Foothills High School, Litchfield Park, AZ

About the Authors

FRED BRAMANTE: THE AUTHOR AS LEARNER

Photo by Bobby Baker Photography.

"High school taught me that I was not very bright. Life taught me that high school was wrong."

Prior to high school, I was a pretty good learner. In fact, in seventh grade, my English teacher, Mrs. Ross, initiated a competition to see who would read the most books by the end of the year. It was a competition that I believed I could win. I won by a mile. I was a reading machine in seventh grade, finishing about 80 books. The second-place winner finished about 50 books. This pretty impressive accomplishment for a seventh grader has resurfaced in a number of aspects of my life, but always on my terms and when I'm ready to engage. However, I am perfectly capable of exhibiting the exact opposite trait.

In eighth grade, I read one book and have averaged less than one book per year during my life past seventh grade. In fact, I read more books in seventh grade than the entire rest of my life. In seventh grade, I felt that I was so smart that I could learn anything. My grades were very good. I made the honor roll fairly regularly, although not high honors.

In eighth grade, things started to slip, and that slip turned into a tumble in high school. My parents pressured me to take the entrance exam for Central Catholic High School in Lawrence, Massachusetts. I remember crying my eyes out, begging them not to make me go to this all-boys, suit coat-and-tie, mega-discipline environment. I know that they wanted what they believed was best for me. My dad never went past eighth grade. My mom never went past her sophomore year in high school. They believed I was bright enough to get into Central and wanted me to try.

I eventually lost the argument and took the entrance exam along with 500 other boys. Two hundred fifty of us were admitted. I remember being proud of the fact that I passed the exam and talked myself into believing that Central would be okay for me, even though all of my friends were going to the local public high school in Salem, New Hampshire (Woodbury High School). For a while, I even became proud of the fact that I was going to Central. While Central and I were not a good fit, I'm not convinced that Woodbury and I, from an academic viewpoint, would have been a better fit.

As a teenager, I was immersed in things that were not conducive to traditional academic studies. Remember, this was the early 1960s. For me, it was surfin,' draggin' (street car racing), rock 'n roll, and girls—and I couldn't get enough.

I was totally into the early years of Dick Clark's *American Bandstand*, the rock 'n roll scene, especially from the late 1950s to the mid-1960s. And, when the California/Hawaii surfing/dragging scene emerged, my mind was filled with thoughts of places 3,000 (California) to 6,000 (Hawaii) miles away. My brain was focused on a soundtrack of the Beach Boys, Jan and Dean, Ride the Wild Surf, Hawaii's Waimea Bay and Banzai Pipeline, Little GTO, Surf City, "two girls for every boy," electric guitars, "she's real fine, my 409," Surfer Girl, and "Fun, Fun, Fun, 'til Daddy takes the T-bird away."

I ate, drank, and slept rock 'n roll. In fact, in order to receive the Holy Sacrament of Confirmation in the Catholic Church, I was required to choose a name of one of the saints as my confirmation name. While most kids were picking John or Mary, I took the name Fabian. Fabian was Pope in 235 AD. Obviously, my choice wasn't made for religious reasons. I picked Fabian because of the 1950s teen idol Fabian Forte. Both sides of the door to my bedroom were covered with the picture sleeves from 45s. (For you kids out there, 45s were musical recordings on black vinyl discs that revolved at 45 revolutions per minute and were played on what we called "record players".)

As the slogan from the movie *American Graffiti* asks, "Where were you in '62?" I was in an all-boys Catholic high school, exactly where I didn't want to be. So what was it like for a kid like me in this high expectations setting? It was torture. And I mean that both literally and figuratively.

Literally, it was an era when the well-known physical abuse of students at many Catholic schools was mostly ignored. While the sexual abuse at Catholic schools during those times became an enormous scandal decades later, the lesser story of those physical abuses has remained untold.

I was basically a good kid who, today, probably would have been labeled with attention deficit disorder. I was never rude. I never got into trouble for swearing, drinking, smoking in the boys' room, talking back, lying, cheating, or fighting. But I did have a bit of class clown in me. I enjoyed talking with my friends and the occasional harmless prank.

For inconsequential reasons, I was physically abused and assaulted by teachers on multiple occasions, including being struck in the face by a Marist Brother during geometry class, breaking my nose. Today, people would be jailed for what went on at my high school.

Figuratively, there were no pretty girls to look at and talk to. In fact, there was almost no one to talk to because there was no talking once you got on to school grounds, except during lunch.

How was a rock 'n roll kid with the confirmation name Fabian supposed to conform to those rules? I remember a social studies lay (nonreligious) teacher telling me that I was going to be a bum. Back then, this was primarily a reference to homeless men who were called bums or hobos. To this day, I can recall where I was sitting, what he looked like, what he was wearing as he said that to me, and the pain I felt when he said it.

How is a teenager supposed to translate being told that he would become a bum, along with being physically assaulted by teachers (I was far from the only one) and having terrible grades on his report card? Isn't the logical conclusion for a teenager that "I'm a loser?" Never once did an adult ask me about my passion for rock 'n roll. Never once did an adult talk to me about what was important to me. While virtually every student in my high school class would have agreed that I was their most passionate schoolmate on the subject of rock 'n roll, no one even hinted that there might be a career opportunity in the music business. I made my living in the music industry for 39 years.

As graduation time approached, I was not sure that I would make it. My grades were terrible. I remember the great sense of relief that I felt, 2 or 3 days before graduation, upon learning that I would be allowed to graduate. It was too late to get a cap and gown, so I didn't walk with my class.

More than 40 years later, I got a better understanding of what probably went on behind the scenes that led to the decision to allow me to graduate. In 2005, I requested a copy of my high school transcript. I found out that, out of my five courses during my senior year, I needed three credits to graduate. My transcript showed that I failed two of the five courses. Sixty-five and above was considered a passing grade. In the three other courses, my highest grade was a 67. My guess is that the school administration spoke to my teachers, asking them to try to find a way to get me to a 65, and that when they secured the three credits, I was notified that I would graduate. Of 212 students in my senior class, I finished number 206; I beat six kids.

My grades were so bad that all four colleges that I applied to rejected my application. My mom told me that I would have a hard time making a living if I didn't go to college. I remember being frightened about my future and thinking, "Why would anyone actually give me money to do something?" In order to improve my grades and reapply to college, I decided to take a couple of night courses at Merrimack College in Andover, Massachusetts. I worked harder than I did in high school and got a C in English and an A in math.

I still wasn't sure what I wanted to do for a career, but knew that I loved being around children, so I thought, "maybe I'll be a teacher." I never even thought about a career in music.

I reapplied to Keene State College, was admitted, and, after 4½ years, graduated (1970) with a 2.3 GPA (grade point average). Fortunately, I majored in general science. With decades of teacher shortages in areas like science, even someone with a 2.3 GPA was able to find a job. I taught for 6 years at Dolan Middle School in Stamford, Connecticut (1970–1976).

After being hired by Dolan's secretary, Tess Manforte, I remember exactly where I was later on that 95-degree summer day on Rt. 91 outside of Hartford, CT, heading back to New Hampshire, where I let out a yell, pumping my fist with joy in my Pontiac Lemans convertible (the top was down). I was so excited that I was going to be a teacher and promised myself that my students would never be bored like I was; that if I made learning fun, my students would learn.

In 1995, Keene State College honored me with their Alumni Achievement Award. In 2006, I got my master's degree in educational leadership from Plymouth State University. In 2009, Plymouth gave me their Alumni Achievement Award. In 1964, both colleges rejected my application for admission.

ROSE COLBY: THE AUTHOR AS TEACHER AND LEADER

My entry into the world of education was a bit unique. Having graduated from college with an undergraduate degree in biology, I was employed as a quality-control microbiologist for a small company that made microbiological media for a period of 2 years. At the point that I knew I wanted a job change, I began looking into education. A local college offered a teacher certification program that I could complete in a summer while also completing the student teaching requirement. Soon thereafter, I became a biology and chemistry teacher at Goffstown High School, in Goffstown, New Hampshire. I always thought that my lack of classical preparation for education was the reason I approached teaching a bit differently than other teachers. With the support of colleagues and more than one administrator, I gained confidence in the classroom in providing an experiential approach to learning biology and chemistry, long before project- and problem-based learning gained prominence.

My skills in the classroom grew solidly over time and were influenced in great part by the work of Bernice McCarthy. 4MAT was the tool I used to hook students into their learning while opening up discovery learning. It was difficult at first to let go of my sense of duty to directly convey all of the content I needed to cover in a short period of time. I became a convert to experiential learning after challenging my students to design and build a model for cell receptor site physiology. They had to figure out how to best represent the binding and activation of a receptor site on the cell membrane that resulted in a change inside the cell. It was the first project I had put out to my students that had them designing the lab rather than my giving them a procedure to follow. The results were stunning. I was as exhilarated as they were on the day they presented their inventions.

When Carol Ann Tomlinson first published her work on differentiated instruction, I felt affirmed. Many of the strategies that Tomlinson outlined in meeting the needs of students were working well for me. I continued to study differentiation and applied the principles of differentiation of process, product, and content extensively.

While deepening my instructional methodologies, my mentor, Dr. Charles Mitsakos, was instrumental in nudging me forward into a leadership program leading to principal certification. Soon after I became the assistant principal of Goffstown High School, the town was building a large middle school to meet the growing needs of the three-town region. After several years as assistant principal of Mountain View Middle School, I became principal.

Mountain View Middle School was clearly a school on the move from its very inception in 1991. Deeply grounded in a philosophy of meeting the unique needs of the adolescent learner, we clearly had put the "junior high" model of schooling behind us. We gave ourselves 5 years to make this transition, and were quite surprised that after the third year of our existence, the beliefs embodied in *Turning Points* were thriving in our school.

In 2002, I was fortunate to be named the Principal in Residence for a leadership project in the state of New Hampshire. During that sabbatical year, I learned a great deal about education and myself. Coaching principals and teachers on projects that advanced student learning brought me into their schools and challenged me to work alongside them to bring clarity and understanding to the change process. That year was formative in deciding that I wanted to move from my career as a principal. My passion in education found my voice!

Throughout my years as a principal, I have served as adjunct professor at Plymouth State University, teaching in the educational administration program. I carried over my lessons learned from the high school classroom to the graduate level with ease. Creating a personal relationship with adult learners, supporting them as they stretch their learning, and counseling and guiding them in decision making is an honor and privilege.

The past 5 years have brought me to many schools as I have worked with teachers and principals to build high-quality competency-based learning and assessment models. This work is cutting edge, difficult, and transformative. It causes many to question their practices in the classroom, their grading practices, and school traditions.

In working with Newfound Regional High School to develop their course competencies, assessment system, and grading philosophy, one of the teachers remarked: "As a teacher, I need to bring my students to competency." How we as educators choose to design a system that brings students to competency will change how we do what we do every day, how we operate our schools, and how our systems of learning work synchronously.

Introduction

Imagine School Without Clocks

Tick tock . . . tick tock . . . We easily fall into the rhythms of time in our lives. We have rhythms for sleeping, eating, working, and playing. We also have a rhythm, bound in time, to school. Most people fall into the rhythm of school from 12 to 16 years or more. For professional educators, the rhythm goes on and on. It becomes so fixed in our thinking that it is resolute, unchanging, and in an odd sense, it's academic. While the world runs on a 12-month calendar, the 10-month calendar is the atomic clock of education.

"Imagine," the signature work of John Lennon's legacy, depicts a rethinking of the world in which the limitations caused by preconceived notions of countries, boundaries, religion, and so forth are gone. Imagine if we could start all over again in our thinking about learning, without the limitations of time.

This piece of rock n' roll history is one of Fred's most prized items in his memorabilia collection. It was given to John Lennon on the release of "Imagine."

Photo by Bobby Baker Photography.

That opportunity to reimagine public education is before us today. At no other time in public education have we been so challenged by the constraints of the economy, the public outcry for changes in financing personnel and resources, and the demand for accountability through testing. In light of the reality of these pressure points, we cannot continue to fund and use our resources as we have in the industrial model of learning.

Imagine if our systems of learning were designed to move our students through achievement and not through time. Time, and not achievement, has been the primary constant of education in the United States. It has been the lynchpin holding in place the 20th century model of public schooling.

Imagine if our systems of regulating, financing, teaching, and learning were not captive to time but, instead: were allowed to occur anytime, anyplace, anyhow, and at any pace: learning in a continuum of mastery.

Our purpose in setting forth this thinking is to engage all stakeholders in the education community—educators, parents, businesses, not for profits, legislators, talented individuals, and, primarily, students—in this conversation, in the deconstruction of existing time-based structures, and in the transformation of learning to a model based on mastery of 21st century competencies.

The primary problem with public education in America is that the foundational structure, in which time is a constant and achievement is a variable, is a fatal flaw that will doom our system of public education to endless mediocrity, regardless of how much money we pour into it. And that mediocrity will translate into failure for our country to produce the educated citizenry necessary to achieve the economic goal of yet another American century.

Creating a system of learning based on mastery and not time will call upon policymakers, politicians, school leaders, educators, and community members to restructure how we can best use our resources in retooling school systems to bring students to mastery.

This book looks at a redefining of public education from two perspectives: one of the policymaker, explaining the hows and whys that caused this new vision for learning to be written into a state's education regulations: and the second perspective of a seasoned, highly skilled practitioner viewing the rulemaking process and implications from the field and, subsequently, implementing change when the vision became official state policy.

As such, the intent of the authors is to assist leaders at local, regional, state, and national levels in playing their personal roles in the transformation of America's system of public education. Importantly, the reference to leaders is not limited to traditional education leaders. While many skilled education leaders are well aware that America needs a new model of public education and are anxious to find tools to help them move education in a new direction, we recognize that there are still too many in public education who wish to protect and defend the public system as it exists; who think that the solutions to America's education problems can be addressed by doing more of what education has asked for and received for decades. Simply stated, their solutions generally revolve around putting more money into the system. The authors recognize that the old proposed solutions of higher taxes, smaller classes, higher salaries, new buildings, more teachers' aides, and the like have been tried and, for the most part, have not succeeded in achieving the high goals of preparing virtually every student with the skills needed to succeed in this global society.

Therefore, our audience reaches beyond school leaders. This audience includes public officials at every level, businesses, community leaders, nonprofit organizations, and most important, parents and students. Even though our paid professional educators are likely to play the most active roles in this transformation, it is our goal to convince America that simply handing the job of educating our students to our educators will no longer be good enough. While our professional educators will coordinate this new process of learning, in order to make this model work, we need to accept that the education of our students will be everyone's responsibility. And yes, we understand that in order for the community at large to accept this shared responsibility, there must be shared benefits.

In this book, you will see where the two voices agree, or even in some cases, disagree. More likely, you will get a well-reasoned look at how New Hampshire has addressed obstacles to transformation, including actual on-the-ground results. Sometimes you will know when it's Fred's or Rose's voice. Sometimes you won't. Oftentimes, the voices will blend. When you are done with this book, we expect your feet to be fully planted in the school transformation camp.

Part I

Leverage: The Perfect Storm

1 Setting the Table for Transformation

Ahh . . . the so-called perfect storm: that coalescence of circumstances that leads to a force never before seen, and it's coming soon to a public school near you. In the past, some of these pressures may have existed, but never with such power and all at once. Virtually unfathomable . . . a Category 6 hurricane.

There is ever-increasing pressure on public education to change. While most educators around the country are keenly aware of the pressure, for many, it is still difficult to envision what it will change into. Most have difficulty envisioning a system that is substantially different than the model that they have known for their entire lives. They still see buildings with classrooms, clocks on the walls, buses that bring students back and forth, textbooks, homework, 180 days, and so on, and so on. So, while the cry for change is loud and clear, for most, the actual picture of what that change could be is very murky—except, of course, in the New Hampshire vision.

Without a logical vision of what to change to, real education redesign will continue to be painfully slow. The proof is borne out in the history of cries for education reform. These cries didn't just start a few years ago. They've been there for decades with failed attempt after failed attempt, to the point that a common phrase among longtime educators is "this, too, shall pass."

"Ya, ya, ya! We know. You want change. You wanted open classrooms, and then you didn't. You wanted new math, and then you didn't. You wanted individualized learning, then you wanted differentiated learning; now you want personalized learning. This, too, shall pass." It's very understandable why many veteran educators feel this way. It's not very different than the story of "The Boy Who Cried Wolf" too often. When the wolf actually showed up, and when the boy cried out once again, many heard the cries but didn't take them seriously.

So, to those skeptics among the education ranks, the reasoning behind this skepticism is understandable. However, to understand the New Hampshire vision and the resulting conversations at the highest levels of America's educational brain trust is to recognize and realize that change is coming. It is real. This change will come so hard and fast that the unprepared may risk becoming casualties.

How can we say with such confidence that this change is coming, that this time the change is real, and that there are no more false alarms? In one word: *leverage*. It's not that there hasn't been leverage in the past, it's that there has never been this perfect storm of leverage. Public education in America is in the early stages of a perfect storm of leveraging forces. When the storm is over, likely within 10 years, we will have a new system of public education that will change how we look at student learning forever and for the better.

THE ECONOMIC IMPERATIVE

In the chambers of our nation's congress, there are virtually no arguments regarding whether America is in an economic crisis, only disagreements on how to cure our financial ills.

Democrats will claim that the $700 billion stimulus package passed in 2009 saved America from a second Great Depression. They claim that it saved our auto industry, saved our banking industry, kept our unemployment rate from going beyond 10%, and saved or created hundreds of thousands of jobs, including jobs in education.

Republicans will claim that the stimulus put America deeper in debt, closer to financial disaster, was a factor in America's credit rating downgrade by Standard & Poor's, and was socialism in action; that the banks and car companies should have had to find a private-sector solution or fail; that we are putting the quality of life for future generations at risk.

In the 2010 elections, it seemed that the Republican arguments won the day. State and local elections swung in a dramatically different direction than the 2006 and 2008 elections in which Democrats won huge victories, including the office of the president of the United States.

So, who's right? The fact is that there's merit in the claims of both sides. And both sides agree, without some dramatic changes in how we do things, the financial stability of our country is in peril.

During the 2008 New Hampshire Presidential Primary, Brian Wallach, a state director for the New Hampshire Obama campaign, then a 28-year-old attorney who took time off from his practice to take a position with the campaign, made the striking comment: "I want to live my life in another American Century."

> *Fred notes: During the 2008 New Hampshire presidential primary, Fred cochaired the state campaign for Mike Huckabee while his wife, Bette, was a member of the Obama team.*

Here we are, in the early stages of the 21st century, with a significant economic lead over other countries, yet if we called Las Vegas to wager on who the economic champion of the 21st century will be, would the United States be the favorite? If America is not the economic champion of the 21st century, is the American quality of life at risk?

On the presidential campaign trail, former Arkansas Governor Mike Huckabee would often ask audiences, "How many of you are living better than your parents?" Virtually all of the hands would go up. Then he would ask, "How many of you believe that your kids are going to live better than you?" Many fewer hands would go up. Are Americans concluding that our best days are behind us? This can't be! We can't allow this to happen. How can we stop this from happening? As President Obama would say, "the fierce urgency of now" is upon us.

The implications from the 2010 elections have been dramatic. While Democrats, from President Obama on down, continue to fight hard to protect public education and argue that America's economic future will be highly dependent on our ability to educate our students, Republicans are looking at every line item, questioning the real value of program after program and even talking about eliminating the U.S. Department of Education. Federal monies to states are being cut, and, in turn, state monies to local districts are being axed. With tremendous pressures at the local level, more and more conservatives are being elected to local school boards to fight for lower property taxes for a cash-strapped citizenry.

At state houses around the country, Republican are challenging collective bargaining rights of unions in order to find precious dollars in what many perceive as overly generous benefit packages. The state house in Madison, Wisconsin (2011), labeled by many teachers' union supporters as Ground Zero, became symbolic of the fight that educators across the country find themselves in.

While we've seen battles over teacher contracts for decades, in most of our lifetimes, we've never seen anything like this. Some estimate that the number of professional educators who will lose their jobs in the next few years will be in the hundreds of thousands, and if so, does that not put even more pressure on public education to transform into something more efficient and more effective or die?

Education has weathered many economic storms in the past. We've seen deep recessions that have forced Americans to modify habits, change lifestyles, and cut back on things that they took for granted. The result, in most cases, had little impact on education. In the tough times of the past, the education community may have been one of the least hard hit. But this economic storm is a big one, and education will not be spared.

If we take huge sums of money out a system that most Americans, Republicans and Democrats, believe is not getting the job done, do we not make an inadequate system worse? Today, economics alone is a force so powerful that the existence of our system of public education, as we know it, is at risk.

While the economics may seem scary to most educators, money problems are the friend of transformation. Without the great financial pressures, public education would likely attempt, once again, to ride this storm out.

THE MORAL IMPERATIVE

Below are excerpts from Bill Gates's 2005 speech to the National Commission on High School Dropouts:

> The more we looked at the data, the more we came to see that there is more than one barrier to college. There's the barrier of being able to pay for college; and there's the barrier of being prepared for it.

> When we looked at the millions of students that our high schools are not preparing for higher education—and we looked at the damaging impact that has on their lives—we came to a painful conclusion: America's high schools are obsolete.

> By obsolete, I mean that our high schools—even when they're working exactly as designed—cannot teach our kids what they need to know today.

> Training the workforce of tomorrow with the high schools of today is like trying to teach kids about today's computers on a 50-year-old mainframe. It's the wrong tool for the times.

> Our high schools were designed . . . to meet the needs of another age. Until we design them to meet the needs of the 21st century, we

will keep limiting—even ruining—the lives of millions of American every year.

Today, only one-third of our students graduate from high school ready for college, work, and citizenship.

The other two-thirds, most of the low-income and minority students, are tracked into courses that won't ever get them ready for college or prepare them for a family-wage job—no matter how well the student learns or the teachers teach.

This isn't an accident or a flaw in the system; it is the system.

The first group goes on to college and careers; the second group will struggle to make a living wage.

Let's be clear. Thanks to dedicated teachers and principals around the country, the best-educated kids in the United States are the best-educated kids in the world. We should be proud of that. But only a fraction of our kids are getting the best education.

We have one of the highest high school dropout rates in the industrialized world. Many who graduate do not go on to college. And many who do go on to college are not well prepared—and end up dropping out.

In the international competition to have the biggest and best supply of knowledge workers, America is falling behind.

That is the heart of the economic argument for better high schools . . . but there's also a moral argument.

Only half of all students who enter high school ever enroll in a postsecondary institution.

Students who graduate from high school, but never go on to college, will earn—on average—about twenty-five thousand dollars a year . . . if you're Hispanic, you earn less. If you're black, you earn even less.

Those who drop out have it even worse. Only 40 percent have jobs . . . nearly four times more likely to be arrested . . . more likely to have children in their teens. One in four turn to welfare or other kinds of government assistance.

But these are our high schools that keep letting these kids fall through the cracks, and we act as if it can't be helped.

It can be helped. We designed theses high schools; we can redesign them." (Gates, 2005)

Bill Gates's 2005 call to action to redesign our schools occurred before we started slashing school budgets across America. In 2005, many were concluding that our schools, especially our high schools, were obsolete, that they needed to be redesigned, but where's the redesign? Have Americans seen a viable, systemic, and systematic redesign of secondary education in the United States? When Bill Gates delivered that speech in 2005, we had no clue that the biggest financial crisis since the Great Depression was a few short years away.

So, if you concluded that we were cheating huge percentages of our kids, as told by Jonathan Kozol's (1991) *Savage Inequalities: Children in America's Schools,* and that we were still cheating huge percentages of our students in 2005 as stated by Bill Gates, what are we to expect for results for our students when huge sums of money are taken out of what most of us see as a woefully inadequate system of public education? As never before, the financial imperative has crashed into the moral imperative. The storm is fierce.

THE GRAYING DEMOGRAPHIC

As Americans live longer, as all of us want to, the consequences of an aging population are getting more and more clear in the health care debate, in the Medicare and Medicaid debates, and, yes, in the local education debates.

With an aging population and reduced percentage of households with school-aged children, it should come as no surprise that many of those grayhairs populate the membership of vocal taxpayer associations whose prime target is what they perceive as the runaway train of school spending. This is not hard to understand. While many are loving grandparents, many are also on fixed incomes. Higher school budgets translate into higher property taxes. For too many of our seniors, we've asked them to make a choice between helping the children of their communities and their personal financial survival. In numerous cases, they live in homes that they have owned for decades, many of which are where they've raised their children. To many seniors, these homes are more than a place to live. They are, in a sense, a significant part of their family. What, in the past, may have felt like a never-ending succession of painful increases in school property taxes is now the primary issue that may cost them their ability to remain in their homes. Seniors vote and vote regularly. Their growing numbers do not bode well for favorable school outcomes at the ballot box, including votes for positions on local school boards.

Never before in the history of our country have we had this phenomenon. The Baby Boomers (post–World War II babies) are starting to turn 65 and will add tremendously to that graying population of retirees on fixed incomes.

Now, add to that a huge percentage of our current teaching workforce among those Baby Boomers who are getting ready to retire. Although many may delay retirement for financial reasons, when they do retire, will they be replaced with younger teachers, or will many of those positions be eliminated? Could these impending retirements be a part of a just-in-time solution?

THE CHANGING STUDENT DEMOGRAPHIC

In addition to the changing demographic of the teaching workforce, there is also a changing demographic in the student population. Due to the prolonged recession, the birth rate has slowed so that, in many areas of the country, pupil populations are shrinking, with the result that teachers are being laid off. Many Millennials are returning to their nests following college, waiting to find employment and trying to make ends meet while paying off college loans. The Pew Foundation (Pew Research Center, 2010) has reported that this boomerang phenomenon has resulted in many Millennials and Gen Xers delaying marriage and/or starting a family. The direct economic effect of this demographic is that the annual cost to educate children in our system presently and in the next few years is rising. The capital costs of running a school building do not decrease if the population housed within it decreases.

TECHNOLOGY

In industry after industry, technology has been a game changer, resulting in both job cuts and jobs added in virtually every industry. In the 1960s, a keyboard instrument called the Mellotron was invented. The concept of the Mellotron was that it would record notes played on stringed instruments, violins, violas, cellos, and basses, one note at a time for each of its keys. So, with 10 fingers, a keyboard player could play up to 10 actual recordings of professional string players playing those notes. You could, therefore, hire someone with a Mellotron to act as a string section for your concert or recording session. The musicians' union was up in arms. They believed that Mellotrons would put musicians out of work.

Today, Mellotrons are in museums. Technology won the war. Today's synthesizers are capable of reproducing far more than just the string sounds of the Mellotron. Virtually any instrument sound is now available on keyboards costing as little as $100.

Did these instruments cost some musicians jobs? In some ways, yes, but in other ways, they made the cost of a performance affordable enough to open doors for other opportunities that may have been previously unaffordable, including lighting, video, live recording, special effects, and so forth. And all of these enhanced opportunities have jobs attached to them.

The emerging integration of technology in teaching and learning in our classrooms is as significant a disruptive force in education as it is in other industries. Many educators attempt to keep a chipper attitude regarding technology and try to position it solely as a great tool in school improvement. Districts boast about their new schools with great technology in every classroom. Yet many of our educators are still struggling to get comfortable with technology, while others feel constrained by local Internet restrictions at the policy level that inhibit full integration of technology-based learning tools.

Today, more sophisticated technology is used by students to support their learning and recreation outside of the classroom, while teachers underuse technology to support learning in the classroom. Our educators must make the most efficient and effective use of technology, even if it totally changes the nature of their roles.

According to Susan Patrick, President of the International Association for K-12 Online Learning, iNACOL, Turkey has created the capacity to serve 15 million students online in 3 years, while, after 14 years, the United States has only 2 million students learning online. But that is changing. iNACOL (2011) projects that by 2019, half of the courses offered in the United States will be online courses. What does that portend for our current learning model?

The studies that compare online learning to traditional classroom learning show that online learning may produce better results than the traditional approach. A meta-analysis of 99 studies that compared student learning in online courses to traditional classrooms showed that "students doing some or all of the coursework online would rank in the 59th percentile in tested performance, compared with the average classroom student scoring in the 50th percentile" and referred to as a "statistically meaningful difference" (Lohr, 2009, p. 1). Students retained 59% of what they were taught in the online format versus 50% in classrooms. The researchers claimed that this was a statistically significant difference (iNACOL, 2011).

In a conversation with Mark Huddleston, President of the University of New Hampshire, he said that they used to make jokes about the

University of Phoenix. Today, they no longer make jokes. The University of Phoenix now has more than 600,000 students. Khan Academy is an online school offering "world-class education for anyone, anywhere." Students engage in short video presentations with ongoing assessment and relearning resources available. Courses are free of charge. Whether in hybrid format to support classroom learning or a total virtual learning environment, the access to web-based learning has moved the notion of technology in the classroom from being standalone hardware and software sets to creating virtual learning communities of learners supported by teachers through personalized learning experiences. The potentially disruptive influence of technology in successfully educating our children at a significantly lower cost can no longer be ignored. As the storm grows, technology will be viewed, by many, as a far less expensive safe harbor.

THE VISION

While the pressure to redesign is great, without having a sense of what that change will look like, we risk a doomed attempt at clinging to a model that we have been comfortable with for too long. Only when a clear vision for public education emerges will stakeholders be willing to move to a new model. This book details the emerging new vision for public education. It is a clear vision with amazing benefits for virtually all stakeholders.

The vision is fairly simple. Instead of time being the primary constant (180 days; 5½ hours of instruction per day; first, second, third, and fourth quarters; Grades 1, 2, 8, 12) with achievement the variable (grades of A, B, C, D, or F), the exact opposite will be the tenets for the new system. Time and place will be the variables and achievement will be the constant.

"That's it?" In large part, yes, but, unless you understand the power that is unleashed when you take off the time shackles, you won't clearly understand the magnificence of this new vision. Herein lies the purpose of this book.

> The vision is fairly simple: Time and place will be the variables and achievement will be the constant.

2 Reform

Getting Better at Things That Don't Work

Twenty-first century learning has been the topic of conferences around our nation. However, in far too many discussions, primary elements that undergird 21st century learning have not been addressed. When brought into the schoolhouse, these 21st century models have become additive to the 20th century status quo. It is like putting a new paint job on a Model T. At a 21st century learning national conference, one of the presenters commented on the work of his organization in saying that "we are getting better and better at things that don't work." Unintentionally, he just defined the problem. The systems underlying what is needed in 21st century learning have not been addressed, yet we have already completed the first decade of the new millennium. We are pouring billions of dollars into trying to get better at things that don't work. The 20th century model of delivering content inside of classrooms during specific times is so highly flawed that it will never work the way it needs to work, but we continue to put in an honorable yet futile effort into trying to make an outdated system better. And, in fact, we are making some gains in some areas. Yet we are only marginally better at things that don't work.

Imagine a plate spinner keeping three plates on poles spinning in the air flawlessly. One plate starts to wobble, and he catches it right away to right it and spin it again. Soon after, another plate wobbles and again he rights and starts it spinning again. Then he notices not one but two plates wobbling. Although more difficult to accomplish, his expertise in plate-spinning skills, perfected over time, puts all three plates spinning again. How successful would he be if all the plates began wobbling at the same time?

We are facing some wobbling plates today in our efforts to reform our schools. Like the plate spinner, we have relied on tried and true skills we have used before to correct the wobble. Are we not at the place in time when all plates are wobbling? The resources we called upon in the past in leveraging school reform efforts are likely not to serve us well in the 21st century.

When standards-based teaching and learning swept the nation in response to state-level assessment testing, teachers tried desperately to fit all the standards into their day-to-day teaching. Many teachers felt the joy of learning was replaced by the race to the end of the year as standards were checked off master lists. Has this reform really worked? Response to Intervention was put forth as a way of meeting learner needs. For schools struggling with resources, this model is becoming more difficult to support over time in multiple content areas. Moving to common core standards may be a move in the right direction in creating our industry standards by identifying the essential learnings, but will this result in high levels of student achievement? How will all other content areas identify common essential standards?

Education has experienced a variety of such reforms. Just think of those reforms that you personally have experienced in your career to date. Can you honestly say that these reform efforts have resulted in each one of your students meeting the anticipated educational outcomes? Can superintendents say that each and every student emerging from Grade 12 has met the educational objectives throughout 12 years of learning? Can high school, middle school, and elementary school principals say that the education children have received when emerging from their schools' levels of learning has prepared each student for the next level of learning? Can grade-level and course-level teachers say that each student has met the targeted learning for the grade or course? At best, we can say that our students have completed years of learning in the educational system; however, we cannot guarantee that they have met mastery of the disciplines along the way.

Educational reform efforts of the 20th century have failed in spite of our ability to move from reform to reform, thinking that we have solved our problem. Yet in education, we rely on the same constructs of teaching and learning that are more than a century old.

DECONSTRUCTION: REMODELING THE PLANE WHILE IT IS IN THE AIR

At a recent seminar on high school redesign, a panel of educators was discussing some futuristic options for framing student learning. Imagine a high school student participating in a course whereby she would attend some regularly scheduled classes, engage virtually through online course-work for other parts of the course, and also participate in a community-based extended learning opportunity that addressed several of the course competencies. In hearing that scenario, a teacher commented that a situation such as this would be impossible to put into a master schedule, especially if the teacher will be overseeing the extended learning opportunity in the community.

This reaction is a normal one. Schedules drive schools—daily schedules, yearly schedules, and examination schedules—all are part of the current framework. In order to move to 21st century learning, we must first begin by deconstructing the elements of the 20th century model of school structure and operation. We must deconstruct the elements of the framework that obstruct the natural process of teaching and learning.

If we ask ourselves how the world we live in currently works relative to time, we would have to agree that it is open for business 24/7. The Internet allows us to interact with work, commerce, and business in some fashion or another through the timeless portal of online communication.

Once time is deconstructed from 20th century learning models, we will be ready to then look at other factors that support student learning. How would our schools use our teaching resources differently if students engaged with teachers in workshop models of learning, problem-based learning scenarios, and virtual learning models?

As we look at the 20th century model of learning, it is based on a deficit model. Students are grouped by age and move together in a cohort through a curriculum. At the end point, some students achieve all of the intended outcomes, many of the students achieve most or some of the outcomes, and some of the students never reach achievement. How would our schools deconstruct that system so that students can move along to mastery at a pace that is appropriate to the learner?

Time, place, resources, and learning models represent points of deconstruction of the 20th century learning model.

RECONSTRUCTION: THE RETOOLING OF LEARNING

Our 21st century learners are not the same learners as the 20th century learners who occupied their seats in our schools. As we will see, our 21st century learners learn differently by virtue of some very organic changes in their brains. The world our learners live in is left at the door stoop of our schools each day. As they walk through those doors, they move back in time to learn in ways that previous generations learned, with materials that often do not meet their discrete learner needs. Our

21st century learners are forced to learn on a schedule, paced to a school year with little regard for their entry level of learning in a class.

We can continue to reform this 20th century model, but we shouldn't think that we will get different results. In order to meet the needs of our learners, we must look very closely at all aspects of our learners' needs.

Reconstruction of our systems of learning must be comprehensive, inclusive, systemic, and systematic. We will be examining each of the aspects of this new thinking as we look closely at how elements of the 20th century model of learning must be retooled for successful reconstruction of public education.

Part II

The New Hampshire Story

Mandating Flexibility: Why Leadership From the Top Matters

First in the Nation! New Hampshire prides itself on its First in the Nation Presidential Primary status. In fact, New Hampshire has a state law that mandates that our primary must be at least 2 weeks before any other state's primary. So if another state decides to move its presidential primary ahead of New Hampshire's, by law, New Hampshire legislators are mandated to move the primary at least 2 weeks ahead of the attempted claim jumping. Yes, it sounds a little obsessive about maintaining this First in the Nation status, but that's New Hampshire.

New Hampshire is a beautiful petri dish for politicians to try to sell their thoughts, opinions, records, leadership qualities, and so forth. New Hampshire is small, ranked 41st in population with 1,235,786 residents and 44th in area. While some criticize New Hampshire as being too white (New Hampshire is tied for third place in this category), it is the fourth-fastest-diversifying state in America. Currently, there are 92 languages spoken in the Manchester, New Hampshire, schools.

This smallness, in both geography and population, that includes true diversity in our larger cities also makes New Hampshire a near-perfect place to, once again, be that petri dish in education redesign. The key players, association heads, Department of Education personnel, school leaders, and state board members, in large part, know each other, see each other, and meet with each other more regularly than they might in larger states where distance becomes a significant factor. Ninety percent of New Hampshire's populations can get to the state capitol, Concord, in an about an hour or less.

This natural advantage of smallness combined with the dedicated participation and pride of being First in the Nation fuels the desire of New Hampshire leaders to build on this legacy. New Hampshire looks for ways to be First in the Nation. Undertaking a full-scale education redesign effort is a natural by-product of the New Hampshire way.

Please note: Public education and politics are inextricably linked. While New Hampshire is a very political state, a conscious effort was made by the authors to ensure that this book would not feel partisan. At various points, we expect that some readers may view the text as having a Republican slant; other passages will sound like Democratic viewpoints.

3 Fred's Story

I left my job as an eighth grade science teacher after 6 years at Dolan Middle School in Stamford, Connecticut (1970–1976), married my English teacher girlfriend (Elizabeth Vasil) in 1976, and moved our family to Salem, New Hampshire, where I grew up and where most of my roots were, in order to pursue my fledgling music business on a full time basis. Daddy's Junky Music had grown from a hole in the wall, $75 a month rent, including utilities (and mice), into a small, on-the-edge-of-respectability, retail chain with four stores in New Hampshire and one in Connecticut. While we were still clearly "junky" (our Stamford, Connecticut, store was located in a challenged neighborhood just a couple of doors from Little Bo's Peeps), in many ways, we were pretty cool and building a following among local musicians.

All of this was happening with my initial investment of $600 and a part-time effort from me. I just had to find out what would happen if I put a full time effort into Daddy's. Although I left teaching as my profession, I have never been able to get the teacher in me out of my blood. In fact, the more successful Daddy's became, and the more accolades I received, both locally and nationally, the more crazed I was over how this could happen to me, to someone that was convinced by school that he wasn't very bright.

So, even though I left teaching in 1976, I never left education. I had this burning feeling that there were lots of kids like me, and maybe they were not so stupid, either. I couldn't stop wondering whether there was a way to remake school so that those kids didn't have to end up in bad jobs or with no jobs. What if they were actually bright in a way that school doesn't see? What if the thing that's truly "stupid" is the way we run schools? I had to know.

I have stayed involved with public education from practically the moment I stopped teaching, pushing in every way I could, trying to find a better way. While my efforts, to many, may have seemed a bit unorthodox, especially my four grossly underfunded and unsuccessful runs for governor of New Hampshire on education platforms, more and more people were recognizing that, although a bit unconventional, I was actually making some sense. Increasingly, I was being looked upon as having a level of expertise at viewing public education in innovative ways. In fact, along with Lee Wilmot, a Republican and local school board member, and Gordon Allen, a Democratic legislator, I even came up with a concept to change the tax structure of New Hampshire. We created a plan and entered the concept (A Flat Tax on Property to Fund an Adequate Education) in the Josiah Bartlett Better Government Awards Competition (1995) and won. In 1999, the concept became New Hampshire law.

In 2002, Craig Benson, a businessman from Rye, New Hampshire, one of the cofounders of Cabletron, Inc., at one point New Hampshire's largest employer, and *Inc. Magazine*'s 1992 National Entrepreneur of the Year, tossed his hat into the gubernatorial ring. Judy Galluzo, who ran one of my campaigns and was now working on Craig's campaign, advised him that he would be well served to sit with me to talk about education. Craig called me to set up a meeting. We met at my home and talked for well over an hour. We got along quite well. He asked me to join his campaign. I told him that I would join the campaign, but I had one request. I told him that if he were elected governor of New Hampshire, he would have the responsibility to name the chairman of the State Board of Education, and that my hand would be in the air putting myself forward for that role. I asked only for the commitment that he watch how I conduct myself during the campaign, get to know me better, and that, if he deemed I was qualified and worthy, he consider me for that position. He said, "That's fair."

Craig Benson was elected governor of New Hampshire in November of 2002. In early 2003, he asked me to chair the State Board of Education.

A key reason I ran for governor is that I believed that there were three government positions in which someone could have a real impact on public education: the governor, the commissioner of education, or the chairman of the state board. While I lost my bids to become governor, in reality, I got exactly what I wanted. In fact, in many ways, I got more. As governor, one would be dealing with virtually every issue, including ground breakings and mall openings, many of which my naturally attention deficit disordered brain would not want to spend a lot of time on. As commissioner, one deals with every education detail, another daunting task. As chair of the state board, most of what one would normally deal with translates into about 5 hours a week, a very manageable task. However, as chair of the board, I put in about 50 hours a week for 2 years, with the clear focus of my efforts aimed at fulfilling the charge given me by Governor Benson, to reform public education.

Governor Benson wanted a businessman/entrepreneur with a passion for education to lead the state board. He wanted real reform because he, like me, was an unsuccessful student. In high school, he was told that he was not college material. He carried that pain with him for a long time. He asked me to help find a way so that kids like we were could be successful. During his inaugural address, he spoke of that painful moment in high school and stated emphatically how he wanted to put an end to tragic stories in which the hopes and dreams of kids are stomped on by the system. My job was to find a way to achieve this honorable goal.

EXPERIENCE COUNTS

Because I had served on the New Hampshire Board of Education in the 1990s, appointed by Governor Judd Gregg, my chairmanship of the Board marked the start of my second term. I had no idea just how well prepared I was for this role.

Prior to that, I had served as chairman of the state's Assessment Steering Committee, which put together the frameworks for New Hampshire's original statewide assessment tool (NHEAP). Simultaneously, the state board had gotten itself into a major fight over the state's school approval regulations called the Minimum Standards for Public School Approval. The issue became so contentious that one board member quit. That left an opening on the state board. Ray D'Amante, a member of the state board, suggested that if the board liked the work that I had done on the Assessment Steering Committee, then maybe they should recommend me to Governor Gregg to fill the vacancy.

Subsequently, I was nominated by Governor Gregg and then, notwithstanding a few bumps, I was approved by the Governor's Council. The most colorful bump was that I was accused of selling Sister Soljah records at my stores (the artist had a controversial record, a single called "Cop Killer"). Fortunately, I didn't sell any records at my stores; we sold guitars, drums, and the like.

I was confirmed and then sworn in on a hot July day in 1992. My first assignment was to go to Exeter, New Hampshire, for a meeting on the Minimum Standards. I knew nothing about the Minimum Standards. I would soon realize how big a deal this document was. I thought, "Who's going to go to an education meeting on a hot day in the middle of the summer?" I arrived at the meeting to find about 300 angry people, furious about what the board was attempting to do with the Minimum Standards. Fortunately, I was pretty innocent in the matter, but I promised the crowd that I would thoroughly look into their concerns.

The next week, the board was to meet in Salem, New Hampshire, on the same subject. In Salem, the crowd was two to three times larger than in Exeter, and they were angry, too. The education community was riled up over what they saw as an overreach by the state board in changing state regulations around numerous issues including class size, libraries, mandated positions, and so forth.

The chair of the state board was Judith Thayer. Judy was very conservative. I mean, *very* conservative. While Judy was more conservative than I am, especially on social issues, she taught me some fabulous lessons. The first lesson was that if you had a bold agenda and you had the ability, the time, and the inclination to pursue that agenda, you could make some pretty amazing things happen from the position of state board chairman.

The second important thing Judy taught me was the significance of the regulatory power in the state boards. In 2009, at a conference on the role of the 21st century educator (Austin, Texas), I heard a presentation by former Rhode Island Commissioner of Education Peter McWalter. He said, "The power is in the State Boards of Education and most of them don't even know it." Oftentimes, including in New Hampshire, a state board chair views his or her primary role as getting through the monthly agenda. That can be a pretty easy gig, completed in as little as 10 hours a month.

In all likelihood, this approach would not be able to capitalize on the available power of the office. For Judy, it was a full-time job without pay.

So, think about it. Judy understood the power of the state board of education, had an aggressive agenda, and pursued it full time. That is a powerful combination.

The third lesson Judy taught me was how not to use that power. Judy evoked, most believed, a pretty heavy-handed approach to changing the regulations, which caused a revolt by the education community.

Because I was the new guy who had nothing to do with initiating the aggressive changes the board was trying to move forward, I was a logical person to try to find a solution to calm things down. I asked Judy for permission to conduct a 1-day meeting to, hopefully, help get to a better place. She granted me that request and, ultimately, the regulations, although with compromises, passed unanimously.

Having been in the center of helping to find a solution, I clearly saw that the newly revamped regulations remained a key component of an outdated system and that, in reality, they needed a far greater revamping than even what the board was trying to accomplish.

BACK TO THE FUTURE

With those lessons learned, I found myself in 2003 in the position of chairman of the New Hampshire State Board of Education with a charge from Governor Benson to reform education. The governor gave me no specific instructions on what he believed reform looked like. Although we often talked of issues, like performance pay for teachers and more choices for kids and parents, he gave me no real marching orders. Frankly, that was the way it should have been. He would say to me, "I want you to go at this with no preconceived notions. Start with a clean sheet of paper."

As the new state board chair, I was the only member on that board appointed by Governor Benson (R). The previous governor, Jeanne Shaheen (D), appointed all six other members. (Governor Shaheen was elected to the U.S. Senate in 2008.)

It was clear that the majority of the state board did not love Governor Benson. Consequently, there was a sense of tension that I was the new kid chairing their board. To complicate things even more, I was telling them that the governor wanted reform, which, in some ways, may have seemed insulting, as if they were twiddling their thumbs before I got there. The early months were not easy and, sometimes, were quite unpleasant.

MY FIRST MEETING AS CHAIRMAN

My first meeting as chairman of the State Board of Education was a landmark meeting in more ways than just "Fred's back." At that meeting, as part of the agenda, the executive director of the New Hampshire School Administrators' Association, Mark Joyce, walked into the state board room with several superintendents of schools. Mark said that they wanted to welcome me back to the state board and to talk to me about the state of affairs around education in New Hampshire, including what they believed was good and not so good about public education in the state.

On their "not so good" list was the subject of charter schools. While New Hampshire had no charter schools at the time, there was much speculation that Governor Benson wanted to push charter schools. Mark said that it was not that the public schools were afraid to compete, but that the playing field was far from level. He said that charter schools have all this flexibility while the public schools have all of these regulations, and that if the public schools were given the same flexibility as charter schools, that the public system would be glad to compete. That statement registered with me and, ultimately, would play a serious role in charting the direction of reform in New Hampshire.

Later, during that first meeting, I talked to the board about creating an action plan to begin the first full-scale education reform effort in the state of New Hampshire since 1919. I talked to them of my previous experience working with the Minimum Standards and said that, while I wasn't sure the Minimum Standards was the right place to start, I was familiar with them and knew that the document was a dinosaur and needed a complete revamping. I told them that, while I was not focusing on of any specific aspect of the document, that I was a 1960s kind of guy who was taught to question authority and that I intended to ask a lot of questions. We then scheduled our first meeting to look at the Minimum Standards for Public School Approval (New Hampshire's K–12 school approval rules).

THE EPIPHANY

Have you ever had an epiphany? Not in a religious sense, but something so jarring that at that specific moment, you knew that your life would change forever?

I had one of those moments at the first meeting to discuss the Minimum Standards. The meeting was held in a small room above the state board of education room. In attendance were members of the state board and members of (then) Commissioner Nick Donohue's cabinet. The meeting was being chaired by (former) State Board of Education member Gail Paine.

Gail started the meeting saying, "Let's get through the easy parts, like the school calendar. We're not going to change anything there." To which I responded, "You might be right that we won't change anything, but I want to talk about it. I know how we got to 180 days and plus or minus 5½ hours of instruction per day. It was so that kids could work in the fields after school and through the growing season. But kids don't do that anymore, so why does it have to be 180 days?"

In the discussion of the 180-day calendar, I asked the group if 180 days was a magic number grounded in research. The answer was obviously no. Our old regulations also called for 5½ hours of instruction a day during those 180 days. I asked the group if there was something special about 5½ hours of instruction. The answer, again, was obviously no. I asked the group whether any of them would care if a district decided to have 5 hours of instruction per day but a longer calendar or 6 hours per day and a shorter calendar? Nobody had any issue with these options.

So we decided to define a school year by simply multiplying 5½ by 180, which came out to 990 hours of instruction. To date, some New Hampshire school districts (i.e. Franklin, Mascenic) have decided to change their calendars. The conversation around rethinking the school year has grown to the point that new legislation has taken the 180 days out of law to provide flexibility to districts as they rethink their own definitions of a school year.

While it may sound like a small change, going from 180 days with 5½ hours per day of instruction to a school calendar based on 990 hours of instruction, this change is far more significant than you'd think. Even though the number of instructional hours offered by schools has stayed the same, the regulations do not call for each student to sit through 990 hours of instruction or even for them to be in classrooms or in the school building during those hours.

But the epiphany happened around high school graduation requirements.

I believe that one of my strengths is asking good questions and, oftentimes, asking the right question is the key to discovering hard to find answers.

I asked the group, "Can someone explain something that I've always been curious about? Why is it that we [the system] give credit to students for successfully completing gym class [their physical education], but if you're on the gymnastics team, you don't get credit?" There was silence around the table. I'm sitting with the highest level of education officials in the state and they can't answer what I believed was a pretty simple question. So I broke the silence. I said that while I don't consider myself an expert, I was a physical education minor in college, and it seems to me that the sports teams demand more hours, a higher level of skill, teamwork, sportsmanship, and that the students who play on sports teams are more likely to continue with physical activity after high school. Isn't that our goal? And, if so, why do we give credit for gym class but not for participation on the sports teams?

Someone responded, "Maybe we should give credit to the kids playing the sports teams." I said, "That's all right with me. Is that okay with everyone else?" Around the table there were shrugging shoulders and nodding heads looking for approval.

Then the next question popped into my head. "What if the school doesn't have a gymnastics team, but there's a gymnastics academy downtown and the exact same lessons and skills that would have been learned if the school had a gymnastics team are going to be taught at the gymnastics academy and you just told me that the students should get credit for learning them? So let's see if I understand this correctly. If the student learns the desired lessons and skills inside the school, it should count toward graduation. But if the student learns the exact same lessons and skills outside the school, that doesn't count. What do we care more about, that the school is the first-hand deliverer of the learning experience, or do we care more that our students learn the desired lessons and skills, regardless of the source of learning?" Every person in the room agreed that they cared more about students' learning, regardless of the source.

I could feel the epiphany coming on. I said, "Okay, music class versus the school band." Someone said, "If the student plays in the school band, they should get credit." I said, "Okay, the student doesn't play in the school band, he or she plays in the local symphony." Someone replied, "That's like the gymnastics academy example. I think that they should get credit if they play in the local symphony." I said, "Okay, the student doesn't play in the local symphony, he or she plays in a rock band." There was more silence around the table. I said, "I'm going to be the defender of the rock bands. I'm not going to tell you that every rock band experience is a great musical experience but . . . a good rock band experience will lead to a lifetime of music making for millions of kids and, in my opinion, that's way more valuable than most music classes." Someone responded, "I'll tell you how I could buy into this. The student goes to the music teacher and says, 'I want to get my music credit playing in a rock band.' The teacher responds, 'Okay, let's put a plan together to make this happen. Here are the state's music standards, what you need to know and be able to do. Let's incorporate this into your rock band experience. Here are my expectations. This is not going to be an easy credit. I want to see significant results. Here's the oversight that I want. Here's how I'm going to assess you, and if you can pass this, I'll give you credit.'" I said, "That's okay with me. Is that okay with everyone else?" Everyone else said, "Yes."

I then said, "A student goes to France for the summer to live with a French family and comes back speaking French. Can he/she get a French credit? Someone said, "Same thing. The student sits with the French teacher, who might say, "Here's a book that I want you to take with you. I want you to spend time on grammar and punctuation," or whatever a French teacher would say. "Let's email each other weekly, and when you get back, here's how I am going to assess your progress, and if you can prove that you've learned what we've agreed on, I'll give you credit." I said, "That's okay with me. Is that okay with everyone else?" Everyone else said, "Yes," to which I responded, "I could do the same thing with every single subject."

Do you see the significance of what this group of high-level state education officials just agreed to? They, in essence, said that, in their view, it's okay for the system to approve, for credit toward graduation, learning that takes place in settings outside of the school and that are not on the school's 180-day timetable. However, they insisted that there must be high standards before the school should give the learning experience its blessing in order to receive credit. This was the origin, the first conversation that led us away from the Carnegie Unit and to a mastery of competencies. . . . Epiphany!!

What I have just described is now translated into regulations in the New Hampshire Minimum Standards for Public School Approval. We mandated flexibility (an oxymoron). New Hampshire has approved, for credit toward graduation, private instruction, online courses, internships, apprenticeships, work study, independent study, sports teams, performing groups, virtually any way students can demonstrate that they have mastered the desired lessons and skills. We refer to these out of classroom offerings as Extended Learning Opportunities (ELOs).

In that one meeting, we concluded that we cared more about students learning than we did about whether the school did the teaching. We concluded that we didn't care where, when, or how the students learned, only that we hold them to high standards before blessing them for credit.

At the end of that meeting, board member Ann Logan, who was not a charter school fan, came up to me and said, "If we do this right, who needs charter schools?" While I don't think our changes in the regulations will eliminate the need for charter schools, in essence, what this does is inject the primary lessons from the charter schools into the public system. Our mantra at the Department of Education became "flexibility and opportunity."

THE NEXT GREAT CIVIL RIGHTS BATTLEGROUND

Governor Benson was well known for stand-up meetings around a tall table. The thinking was that standing up made meetings shorter and more focused. One day I went into his office and said, "Governor, I think you're going to need to sit down for this meeting." His eyes widened and he asked, "Is everything okay?" I said yes but explained that I was not sure whether he was going to love or hate what I had to say.

We sat down and I said, "Everyone knows and accepts that kids learn in a variety of ways and have different learning styles." I talked about the brain research conducted on how people learn. He agreed. I continued, "Everyone accepts that some of those learning styles work well in traditional classroom environments, but, for many students, that environment doesn't work." He, again, agreed and said that it works well for about one third of students and reiterated that it didn't work well for students like we were. I then said, "If we agree that the traditional classroom model does not work well for a large percentage of our students, yet 95+% of our delivery model is the traditional classroom, do we not have a system that favors those kids who learn well in that environment and discriminates against those students who do not learn well in traditional classrooms?" The governor's eyes widened and he said, "Fred, be careful how you use that word [*discrimination*]." (Historically, claiming discrimination has not been a cry from the right side of the political spectrum.) I told him that I understood his concern but believe that this foundation structure of our education system, the traditional classroom, should become the basis for the next great civil rights battleground.

Governor Benson told me that if he could get past his upcoming bid for re-election, he and I would talk of the possibility of holding a press conference declaring the traditional classroom, especially at the high school level, the civil rights issue of our time, not on the basis of race, creed, gender, or sexual orientation, but on the basis of how students learn. I believe that, if this had been done by a conservative Republican governor of an influential (First in the Nation Primary) state, this would have been national news.

But Governor Benson lost his bid for re-election to John H. Lynch, so the press conference never happened. With the new governor came a new commissioner of education, Dr. Lyonel Tracy, and a new chairman of the New Hampshire Board of Education, David Ruedig.

TRANSITION TO A NEW ADMINISTRATION

I was very disappointed at Governor Benson's loss. I had put in 50 hours a week for 2 years on what we called "Real World Learning." Was it all about to go away? Along with a new governor and new commissioner of education often comes a new direction, a new vision for education. I had no idea what would happen with our groundbreaking efforts.

Poster promoting Real World Learning, New Hampshire's new direction in public education (2004)

Poster created by Kathi DiSesa. Photo by Bobby Baker Photography.

While the board had finished its work on the Minimum Standards, the document had not yet been fully approved by the Joint Legislative Committee on Administration Rules (JLCAR). So much hard work had gone into this project. Personally, I had never worked harder on anything in my life. Were my last 2 years and 5,000 hours of effort about to go down the drain?

The night prior to the hearing before JLCAR, I found out that the New Hampshire School Administrators' Association (NHSAA) had written a letter to JLCAR encouraging them to vote "no" on the proposed rules changes. To say the least, I was very unhappy with the administrators. Their executive director, Mark Joyce, told me more than a year ago that Dr. Darryl Lockwood, their representative on the Standards Task Force, a yearlong, very inclusive effort in shaping the regulations, "speaks for me." Darryl and the NHSAA team had signed off on the proposed changes to the Minimum Standards twice. While the school administrators caused more changes in the various drafts than all other participating organizations combined, they now had yet another objection, the removal of the Carnegie Unit. In my view, after the organization had signed off twice, its letter to JLCAR was unprofessional.

Newly appointed Commissioner Tracy arrived at the JLCAR hearing and told board member Debra Hamil and me that he was there to support us. He approached Mark Joyce in the hallway outside the hearing room at the Legislative Office Building and, in no uncertain terms, let Mark know that he was there to dispute Mark's letter.

Dr. Tracy was the first to testify. He did a great job refuting the letter from the administrators, and, after his convincing testimony, it was pretty much a done deal. The rules passed.

While the school administrators objected to the removal of the Carnegie Unit, I must admit that, to date, they have been much more supportive than I thought they'd be. While not every superintendent in New Hampshire is fully on board with the new regulations, more and more are, and the NHSAA under Mark Joyce's leadership has been quite supportive in getting its members more comfortable in understanding and dealing with the challenges of this new direction. However, we still have a long way to go.

FOLLOW THE CHILD

While Dr. Lyonel Tracy was instrumental in getting the new rules passed through the JLCAR process, he did come to the Department of Education with his vision. He called it *Follow the Child*. Follow the Child? What about what we called Real World Learning? Is it now over? Lyonel had been working with Dr. Russ Quaglia and the Quaglia Institute for Student Aspirations on this concept that focused on a personalized learning experience for every student. Well, that sounded pretty good to me. But how is this different than Real World Learning? Dr. Tracy's approach was a whole-child approach, not simply academics, but also the personal, social, and physical aspects of educating students. Well, that sounded good, too! But what does this mean for Real World Learning, where learning can happen anyplace, anytime, in or outside of schools?

It was spring and baseball season was upon us. I knew that Lyonel was a player in high school and a Red Sox fan (fanatic, actually), so I felt that asking him to bring his glove and ball to play catch on the DOE lawn after our state board meeting would help break the ice so that we could talk of my concerns. I had often played catch with former Commissioner Charlie Marston during my term in the 1990s. Lyonel was looking forward to playing catch and so was I.

Knowing that we would have some leisure time after the Board meeting, I wanted to plan my conversation with him. In the summer, my boat on Great Bay (New Hampshire) serves as my office. My wife refers to me as a Zen boater. Basically, I drive to the middle of the bay, shut off my motor, and let the tide take me wherever it wants. Occasionally, a fish will jump and break my train of thought, but, for the most part, it's amazingly tranquil. On my boat, I decided to create a flow chart of what I thought a Follow the Child system of education might look like.

On a beautiful New Hampshire day, after the State Board of Education meeting, Lyonel and I took off our ties, got out our gloves, and went out on the department's lawn. After a good game of catch, as we were putting our gloves back into our cars, I brought out the flow chart and told Lyonel what I had done and asked him to follow my logic to see if this fit his Follow the Child thinking.

I said to him, "If we're supposed to follow the child, doesn't that mean that the child is the leader of his own education?" Lyonel said, "Yes." I responded, "Well then, doesn't that make us, the educators, the parents, the followers of the child, basically, the child's support team?" Lyonel said, "Yes." I responded, "Then we're on the same page."

Ultimately, I really didn't care a lot about whether we called it Follow the Child or Real World Learning. I cared about creating a new system for public education that was not built around time but was built around a customized/personalized education for each student.

THE VISION DOCUMENT

After passing the new regulations (Minimum Standards for Public School Approval, 2005), in 2006, New Hampshire began the process of creating a vision for high school redesign. A group of 21 education leaders came together to develop a document that was to bring light to the spirit and intent of the changes that were made to the Minimum Standards and to guide our educators in actualizing the model envisioned in the new regulations.

We were working on this project with U.S. DOE planning grant monies that we had received after numerous meetings and conservations with Assistant U.S. Secretary of Education Dr. Susan Sclafani. Dr. Sclafani wanted to make sure we were serious about making credit available for all subjects, not just electives. When she saw we were serious, she approved the grant.

On the suggestion of Paul Leather, the group's leader (current Deputy Commissioner of the New Hampshire DOE), we sought outside consultants to help us craft the document. I was always a bit wary of an outsider coming in to help us shape our vision, one that was, likely, very different than anything that they had seen before, into a document.

Many months into the process with lots of hard work from the committee, and three consultants later, we found ourselves in a difficult position. We finally received a draft of the document from our third consultant and it was, in my opinion, unacceptable. It included education clichés that we've heard for decades and pictures of kids in schools that we've seen for decades and did not capture the direction that was reflected in our new rules. It seemed to me that every place it said *New Hampshire* in the document could have been replaced with any other state and nobody would know the difference. It depicted, in my opinion, a 20th century delivery model. I was unhappy. This was very understandable to me. We were going to a place no other state had gone before.

I made some calls to other members and they echoed my sentiments, that the draft did not reflect what we were envisioning. I called Paul Leather the night before our group was to meet and told him how displeased I was and that I intended to make a motion to start over. Paul was not happy. He expressed concern that we were running out of money for this project and that he believed we could rework the document into something the group could be satisfied with. I rarely disagree with Paul because I know how deeply he cares about moving redesign forward, but this was one of those times.

The next day, the group gathered. Paul opened the meeting and I immediately raised my hand. I told the group that our consultant didn't understand the basic essence of our direction, that the draft document needed to be totally scrapped, and that we needed to start over. I then pointed to members of our committee and said he or she "gets what we are trying to accomplish, but our consultant doesn't." I then said, "Give it to me. I'll do it for free. I'm not telling you that I want to do this, but at least I get it. So, give it to me. Now, if others want to work with me on this, I'd really appreciate that."

Our deputy commissioner, Dr. Paul Ezen, was the first to raise his hand. He said, "I'll work with Fred on it." Next was DOE member Sue McKevitt, followed by Superintendent of Schools (then Kearsarge, now Manchester) Dr. Tom Brennan.

So, the four of us took on the primary responsibility of drafting the document. After numerous meetings at Paul Ezen's house and even one on my boat, within a couple of months, we brought back our draft to the committee. With minor tweaking from the committee, it was agreed to send it to the State Board of Education for approval.

At the state board meeting, board chairman David Ruedig made a very important contribution to the final document. He remarked that the document was not strong enough on the subject of moving the teaching profession to less full-time classroom delivery and more facilitation of the process of learning.

Board member Dr. Daphne Kenyon expressed her feeling that the document did not speak with a consistent voice and insisted that a professional writer be hired to improve the readability of the document. The board also asked for an opening letter from Commissioner Tracy.

The changes were made and the document was now complete. In 2007, *New Hampshire's Vision for Redesign: Moving From High Schools to Learning Communities* made its public debut (New Hampshire Department of Education, 2007). The following table outlines New Hampshire's methodical efforts to align the pieces to move away from the Carnegie Unit to an anytime, anyplace, competency-based system of learning.

Table 1 Timeline of Significant Events in Moving Away From Seat Time

2002	"One in Four," New Hampshire Center for Public Policy study says 25% of New Hampshire students drop out of high school
2002	Election of Craig Benson as governor of New Hampshire
2003	Appointment of Fred Bramante as chairman, New Hampshire State Board of Education
2003	New Hampshire initiates first statewide school reform effort since 1919
2004	Election of John Lynch as governor of New Hampshire
2005	Adoption of new Minimum Standards for Public School Approval
2005	Lyonel Tracy replaces Nick Donohue as commissioner of education
2005	Governor Lynch holds first New Hampshire Dropout Summit
2006	Nick Donohue named president and CEO of Nellie Mae Education Foundation
2006	"Now, One in Five," New Hampshire Center for Public Policy study says 20% of New Hampshire students drop out of high school
2007	New Hampshire raises dropout age to 18
2007	New Hampshire Vision for High School Redesign
2008–2009	Last school year that credit for seat time (Carnegie Unit) is available in state regulations
2009–2010	First school year that all credits toward graduation must be based on mastery of required competencies
2010	Virginia Barry replaces Lyonel Tracy as New Hampshire commissioner; Paul Leather named deputy commissioner
2010	New Hampshire Board of Education approves Competency Validation Tool for field use
2011	New Hampshire's cumulative dropout rate is 4.68%
2011	New teacher training regulations New educator-development regulations More modifications to K–12 regulations
2012	Goal for dropout rate to be 0

4 Rose's Story

The moment of epiphany experienced by Fred and his subcommittee members of the Board of Education translated into confusion and misunderstanding by teachers and administrators. Fred appeared in many venues explaining, with great passion, how kids will be vested in their high school education when they are able to make decisions about how, when, and where, they could engage in their learning. Fred spoke to parents, teachers, administrators, and professional organizations and at community meetings around the state.

In some places, his message was met with disdain—"I can't believe kids will get credit for taking a vacation to France!" "I can't believe kids will get credit for playing in a rock band!" Clearly, the shock value of hearing those possibilities had teachers and administrators thinking of all of the reasons why these things couldn't possibly work.

How do you systematize this wild thinking? If kids can earn credit for playing sports or belonging to a gym, we won't need physical education teachers anymore! If kids are learning a world language while on vacation, we won't need as many world language teachers! The high school world was abuzz with conjecture, denial, and, in some circles, a "this too shall pass" attitude. Many members of Fred's audiences never listened to him beyond his vision-setting opening message. I heard Fred speak to several different audiences during that time. He always delivered the message that students receiving credit for real-world learning would do so with the direction of qualified teachers, earning credit with demonstration of competency. It was this part of the message that had the greatest implication for transforming learning, yet many educators didn't really understand its meaning.

Once the board had developed the first draft of the Minimum Standards document, the New Hampshire Department of Education created a task force group of teachers, principals, and superintendents to work on bringing the document into a final form for its final approval process by the New Hampshire Board of Education. While serving as the president of the New Hampshire Association of School Principals, I was asked to serve on this task force. Also as a member of the New Hampshire Department of Education's Professional Standards Board, I took a keen interest in the work of this task force. The group met many times over several months. Some areas of these new standards were easy to work through, while other sections were labor intensive. There seemed to be a continual tension between developing some key standards that promoted district-level decision making relative to most phases of school operation while, at the same time, trying to keep a regulatory rein in order to create equity of opportunity in the school districts across the state.

New Hampshire prides itself on local control of education. The task force was very mindful that a change in any standard might create an unfunded mandate by the state to the local district. Such language would prompt legal challenges. At the time, there were several districts that did not have public kindergarten. New Hampshire was the only state in the country that did not have mandatory kindergarten. The draft document of the new standards dealt with requiring kindergarten in all districts as well as changing the restrictions of school calendars to give flexibility of the districts to schedule school, defining the number of hours in the school year for elementary, middle, and high school levels.

The section of the rules relative to earning high school credit through extended learning opportunities (ELO) was discussed at length. Most members of the task force were on board with the philosophy of ELOs but struggled with how to systematize and institutionalize it. There were questions about how the ELO work would be regulated and overseen at the state level.

The task force completed its work by sending its final version forward in the approval process. The 2005 final version of the New Hampshire Minimum Standards for School Approval represented forward thinking by members of the educational community.

Most school leaders in the state were connected with the new and controversial rules contained in the Minimum Standards document. The New Hampshire Commissioner of Education, Lyonel Tracy, and the Deputy Commissioner of Education, Mary Heath, met monthly with the board members of both the principal and superintendent associations in the state throughout the process. Those school leaders who were looking at the new standards for the first time in 2005 were clearly shocked by the implications of the new rules. Others who had been connected with their professional organizations and those who had been having ongoing conversations along the way about the new rules were ready to move forward to explore new possibilities.

REALITY CHECK: WHAT IS A COMPETENCY?

The rules relative to competencies, assessment systems, and extended learning opportunities became the focus for many professional meetings and conversations. High school principals in particular reached out for understanding of the implications of these rules in order to lead their school communities through this change. The New Hampshire Association of School Principals, led by Executive Director Peggy McAllister, created network meetings around the state for principals to gather, learn, discuss, and, yes, complain about the rule changes.

At the heart of these discussions was the real question: What is a competency? How many competencies should a course have? How do you assess a competency? The conversation and buzz about these key questions went on for almost 2 years leading up to the 2008 to 2009 school year deadline for adoption, when the competencies must be put into place.

During this time, several opportunities for shaping this understanding were taking place with grant support to several schools and the leadership of the New Hampshire Department of Education. The high schools who were the early adopters in developing competencies shared their work at a statewide conference, which gave more schools confidence to move their work forward.

The interest and passion for real-world learning also brought together teachers and administrators from across the state to learn from each other through conferences.

FLAVOR OF THE MONTH?

In education, we often move from wave to wave of new thinking. Teachers often refer to this as "flavor of the month" professional development. Teachers in schools that experience frequent turnovers in leadership are often most vulnerable to the "out with the old, in with the new" wave of change in their schools and districts. This has a numbing effect on professional staff by damping down their enthusiasm for anything new coming their way. They often learn that the hours of work put into an initiative are often laid waste, so they opt instead to just let it pass. Was all this fuss about competencies another flavor of the month?

Other than a few opportunities to network between school leaders, there was little guidance offered in 2005 and 2006 for the development of competencies. A competency became a self-defined entity. In some schools, there was summer professional development time afforded to high school staff to gather and "git 'er done." The result of this effort was great variation from discipline to discipline in the quality and number of course competency statements.

Coming from a content-rich, traditional instructional delivery, many teachers simply sat down, opened up the textbook, and listed all of the important information students needed to exit the course knowing. Little attention was paid to assessment because teachers felt that the traditional written test at the end of the chapter met the criteria for the required assessment of competencies.

At the other extreme, some schools approached the writing of competencies based on good curriculum design. There had been quite a bit of training in the state in the Understanding by Design (UbD) model over the course of several years. Some high schools had created their course templates and assessments using this model. These schools went back into that work to create the course competency statements in each discipline.

GOOD IDEA GONE BAD?

Two years after the Minimum Standards were in effect, the picture was looking pretty grim. Some schools wrote competencies to simply meet the new standards. Other schools were developing and evaluating their competency statements over time. And still there were others that were waiting for all of this to just pass by them that had not even begun to write course competencies or assessments.

In June 2006, having retired from my principalship, I associated with the Capital Area Center for Educational Support (CACES), at the request of Dr. Kenneth Greenbaum, to develop competencies in the area of science, my area of certification.

We decided to ask the best and brightest science teachers in the state to come together to develop course exemplars. We chose to create a cohort for biology, chemistry, and earth science. At the outset, Ken felt that it was a colossal waste of time and money for teachers in each high school to sit and write competencies when we could accomplish the same thing with a small group of teachers, then use technology to share the work throughout the state. We created a collaborative of school districts, which paid a minimal cost ($1,000) to join. They would then receive the passkey for a Moodle website. We loaded many documents on the Moodle server as resources for teachers. When a school district joined the collaborative, it could take the exemplar courses and then adjust them to suit its needs, and then upload its version of the courses for others to share.

In preparing for this work, we wanted to create a common template for all to use. In an effort to be comprehensive, I reviewed the science standards for each of the 50 states. Throughout that process, I was looking for states that had anything to offer us relative to competencies and assessments. After this exhaustive research, I realized there were none. Indeed, we were the pioneers. However, there were three models that were intriguing: Hawaii, Georgia, and the District of Columbia.

As a curriculum and assessment specialist, I knew we would be using the Understanding by Design (UbD) framework as our model. We developed an approach to the design of competencies that was in keeping with the design of high-quality, enduring understandings. It was in this phase of development that we came to the unequivocal definition of competency: Competency is a student's ability to transfer his/her learning in and/or across content areas.

We looked to Hawaii for the format of the document. The District of Columbia documents led us to the creation of engaging scenarios to provide the exemplar for authentic performance assessment. Georgia's model represented a more thematic or conceptual approach in its curriculum mapping. Both Georgia and the District of Columbia utilized the UbD framework to inform our work since they had created curriculum documents for each of the science areas.

As the exemplars were developed and shared, our work soon became known as the CACES model. As the work became known across the state, the New Hampshire Department of Education asked that we develop exemplar course documents in the other content areas. We reached out to each of the professional associations in the content areas to suggest their best and brightest teachers to participate in this work. Using the same template, we again published all of the work on the Moodle server to be shared by schools in the collaborative.

Although the New Hampshire Department of Education supported and showcased the CACES model, it was not in the position to require that all school districts use the model. Indeed, by that time, many schools had moved their competency work forward. For others, the exemplars afforded them the opportunity to revise their work, to choose not to use the CACES model, or to simply download any course model they wished to use or adapt.

In 2007, CACES was asked to become a partner in a project, funded by the Nellie Mae Education Foundation, in conjunction with the New Hampshire Department of Education, Kim Carter of the Q.E.D. Foundation, and PlusTimeNH, a former nonprofit organization supporting after-school programming. The Nellie Mae Education Foundation (Quincy, Massachusetts) is led by former New Hampshire Commissioner of Education Nick Donohue. CACES would guide schools in their development of course competencies while providing support for building a model for student success in extended learning opportunities. Newfound Regional High School, Laconia High School, Franklin High School, and Manchester

High School Central were chosen as the schools we would be working with to develop the competency-based extended learning opportunity model. Over the course of 3 years, the project partners provided onsite monthly support for the school leaders, ELO coordinators, and teachers involved in this work. Other high schools joined the partner schools in creating a network of schools beginning to provide extended learning opportunities to their students. Because this was a research-oriented project, data were collected on all students participating in extended learning opportunities. At the same time, we learned from each other as the work moved forward. The highlight of this work was always to witness the students demonstrating their learning from their ELO coursework.

By 2009, there was a growing frustration at the board of education level as well as within the ranks of the superintendents. The world of competencies and real-world learning was not turning out quite the way it was envisioned. The language in the minimum standards relative to competencies, assessment, and mastery was vague enough that schools could pretty much choose to do what they wanted to with it. There was growing pressure for the New Hampshire Department of Education to write competencies for each course at the high school level in order to move everyone in the right direction. Yet many schools had really done admirable work in this area.

It was decided that CACES would facilitate the work of a group of teachers from high schools throughout the state who had developed different competency and assessment models to create a competency-validation tool. Teachers could examine their competency statements using this rubric. We drew heavily from the Nellie Mae project partner schools because they had worked extensively in the development of their course competencies. We used the best practices in curriculum and assessment put forth by Wiggins and McTighe, Erickson, Stiggins, Marzano, and Reeves. The group created a tool that would measure the strength of a competency based on its enduring nature, its relationship to content area standards, its assessability, and its cognitive demand.

The group knew that this tool needed to pass tests for both validity and reliability. We used Stiggins's metarubric (Stiggins, Arter, Chappuis, & Chappuis, 2009) for good rubric design and created the Competency Validation Rubric (CVR) over several sessions. Each participant from each school was then charged with taking the CVR back to his or her school and testing it out with teachers from various disciplines against at least 50 competency statements. Each school then reported back on the reliability of the tool with suggested language changes for the second version of the CVR. Spaulding High School held an in-service day whereby each department used the tool to validate its course competencies, giving us feedback and suggestions for language changes to the CVR.

The Competency Validation Rubric was presented to and approved by the New Hampshire Board of Education on April 14, 2010. The work was welcomed by the board as a tool to assist school districts in the development of high-quality competencies. The Competency Validation Rubric would also be used by members of the New Hampshire Department of Education in assisting schools with their school approval process.

HOW DO YOU GRADE COMPETENCY?

A high school student must demonstrate mastery of course competencies in order to gain credit. The minimum standards were quite clear in that expectation. However, it was equally clear that the traditional way in which we give credit to students draws heavily on the way we document learning using the Carnegie Unit. At issue was the fact that students were continuing to receive credits for earning a grade of 60, or 65, or 70. The word *mastery* sounds great qualitatively and philosophically, but how is mastery interpreted quantitatively?

The mushroom cloud could be seen on the horizon! The last bastion of traditional high school was beginning to fall. Schools realized they had to change their report cards to a competency-based report. The implications of this were actually more far reaching than the original move to competency-based courses.

It was clear that teachers, parents, and society in general do not recognize a grade of 60 or 65 as a point of mastery for anything. How could we then give high school credit for that grade? Even if a course had well-defined competencies and assessments, if the school district policy awards credit for a course for an earned grade of 61 or 66 or 71, the school district was making a de facto declaration that 61 or 66 or 71 represented mastery.

Sometimes we learn best through other people's suffering, and this was true for competency-based report cards. In its first year of existence, a newly built high school chose to use a traditional report card to report student progress. At the end of the year, the teachers created a report on course competencies. Unfortunately, many students who received grades of A or B in their courses also had to go to summer school because they failed one or more competencies for the course. The parents and public were in an uproar. How could that be?

This situation forced high schools to take a long, hard look at their method of reporting on student learning and also to examine what would be the "set point" with which they were comfortable in declaring mastery of competencies.

Rob Lukasiak, a fellow CACES consultant in competency-based development and assessment, joined with me to create a competency-based-learning grading model. We worked with many schools throughout the state to facilitate their conversations in moving toward a system that communicated mastery of course competencies. Each district had its own approach as well as limitations (mostly because of technology) in how it embraced this work. We drew from the work of Guskey, O'Connor, Wormeli, and Marzano (see Appendix) so that schools would use the best practices. Guiding staff through study and research on these best practices lead to the development of grading philosophy statements, which complemented their competency and assessment models.

This model presented the unpacking of competencies into a set of performance indicators designed to Webb's Depth of Knowledge levels. Summative assessments at Levels 3 and 4 of the Depth of Knowledge would represent at least 80% of the final grade, with formative assessments representing 20% or less of the final grade. Reassessment opportunities to bring students to competency, elimination of the 0, and separate reporting of effort, motivation, and behavior were included in most grading philosophy statements.

In essence, a course grade would communicate student achievement or mastery of the course competencies. Although it would be nice if a school had the ability to report achievement on each course competency, most student information systems in use lacked the sophistication to do so.

Of all of the work in the development of a competency-based learning environment, the work in developing competency-based grading systems came closest to day-to-day teacher practice and, as a result, has become the tail that wags the dog. When it comes to how a teacher enters grades in a grade book, it requires a change of practice. When grades are not entered by format of the assessment (test, quiz, project) but rather by the competency for which the assessment was designed, a new picture of student achievement emerges.

The work in reshaping grading practices has been transformative for both teachers and students. High schools that have begun working with grading system reform understand the need to use an open system of communication with students and parents. The work is ongoing and developmental in many high schools.

5 New Hampshire Present and Future

Is public education in New Hampshire already in the 21st century? In reality, not yet. Probably more so than any in other state, New Hampshire has one foot solidly in each century but is clearly putting more and more weight on the front foot as it steps into the 21st century.

WHERE IS NEW HAMPSHIRE NOW?

Some examples of New Hampshire's emerging 21st century learning model include:

- State Education Regulations revamped in 2005—New Hampshire is probably farther ahead here than any other state. The Carnegie Unit (credit for seat time) has been eliminated and high school credits, theoretically, can only be acquired when students demonstrate mastery of required competencies (2009–2010).
- Virtually every high school has completed its competencies for virtually every course.
- Regulations allow credit for learning anytime, anyplace, anyhow, and at any pace.
- Extended Learning Opportunities (ELOs) can be approved for credit toward graduation for private instruction, online courses, independent study, internships, work study, and other community-based learning opportunities with local mentors.

- *ELOs, personalized,* and *competencies* are cemented parts of New Hampshire's education vernacular.
- ELO coordinators are among the fastest-growing positions in public education in New Hampshire.
- An IHE (Institutions of Higher Education) Network has been formed by all of New Hampshire's teacher training institutions to rethink educator development for the 21st century.
- Two annual summits on 21st century educator development have taken place (2010–2011).
- New teacher training regulations are now in place (2011). In large part, the word *teacher* has been replaced by *educator, classroom* has been replaced by *learning environment,* and *instruction* has been replaced by *learning* or *learning strategies.*
- State law and regulations now allow changes in school calendars (180 days is no longer required by the state).
- High school dropouts are nearing extinction; New Hampshire's cumulative dropout rate has fallen from 25% in 2002 (Hall, 2003) to 4.68% in 2011 (New Hampshire DOE, 2012). New Hampshire has targeted 2012 for the elimination of dropouts.
- Many districts have instituted standards/competency-based report cards.
- Many high schools have standardized course grading practices by creating grading philosophy statements. Grades for courses reflect mastery instead of a mix of indicators found in the traditional course grade (effort, motivation, attendance, homework).
- New Hampshire's Virtual Learning Academy (VLACS) is now the state's largest public school.

While New Hampshire's list of 21st century exemplars is impressive, the Granite State has a long way to go. Below are indicators that New Hampshire's back foot is still in the 20th century:

- The vast majority of learning in New Hampshire's schools still takes place in traditional classrooms.
- The regulatory changes are still primarily an "inside baseball" conversation. Only a small percentage of New Hampshire's' population understands the new regulations and their implications, including students and parents.
- Most schools still allow Cs, Ds, and Fs as grades. In a mastery-of-required-competencies system, how are these grades possible? They are possible because most schools are still using time-based calendars without due regard for consistent grading practices by teachers in determining student achievement and mastery.

- Teacher training, while probably more informed on the need to change than in any other state, in large part is still in the 20th century, training standalone teachers for standalone classrooms. However, in many IHEs, things are already changing.
- Many elementary and middle schools have focused on standards-based learning as part of school improvement initiatives, yet learning is still bound to the traditional school calendar and school pace.

WHERE IS NEW HAMPSHIRE GOING?

Education in New Hampshire is a moving target. As the ink is drying from our writing, there is so much going on in New Hampshire that, in all likelihood, much will have changed by the time this book hits the streets. But if the authors had waited 6 months or a year, they would be in the same situation. While the pace of school transformation in America is moving at varying speeds, from relatively quickly to painstakingly slow, in New Hampshire, from a statewide view, the pace is very fast. To date, there has been very little backlash from the system, but that inevitably will change as the implications of transformation begin to impact collective bargaining issues, which they clearly will.

Moving Away From Time

With changes in state laws and regulations allowing districts to change their calendars, some have begun to do so. For example, the Mascenic School District, under the leadership of Superintendent Dr. Leo Corriveau, has already changed its calendar to 175 days with an additional 22 minutes per day. Mascenic was doing block scheduling with four 85-minute blocks per day. In the new schedule, an additional block was added, but the blocks were shortened to 72 minutes, thus, giving teachers a full 72 extra minutes per day to collaborate, meet with students, meet with community partners, plan, and so forth. This was bargained with the local union, and so far, so good. Mascenic is not a wealthy district. In fact, by New Hampshire standards, it's a property-poor district, meaning fairly low per-pupil spending with high property tax rates. Yet every school in the Mascenic district met A.Y.P. in 2010.

While Mascenic's calendar change is showing positive results, as in districts across America, teachers are still paid for time, for working a fixed calendar. But as time measures inevitably erode and more districts take advantage of regulatory flexibility, there will be more focus on performance measures. Teacher pay will become more and more of an issue as a competency-based system will ultimately challenge the basic, century-old "pay for time" compensation system.

Seniority and Tenure

The tenure law (Senate Bill 196, June 2011) in New Hampshire has recently been reformed, making it harder to attain continuing contract status and making it easier to non-renew a teacher on continuing contract. However, as more and more students and parents understand that they have more choices than ever before, the issues of seniority and tenure will become virtually moot. For example, if a classroom teacher with 25 years of experience in a district that is offering growing numbers of options for students, either online or in real-world settings, is now struggling to attract students, tenure and seniority won't mean much of anything without student demand for his/her services.

IHE (Institutions of Higher Education) Network

At the first New Hampshire Summit on 21st Century Learning, an ad hoc group of statewide education leaders, nicknamed "the Summiteers," who attended a similar national summit in Austin, Texas, in 2009, brought together teams from 14 of New Hampshire's 15 teacher-training institutions. In the opening remarks of the summit, Dr. Robert McLaughlin, the leader of the Summiteers, stated that one of the goals of the summit was to form an IHE network so that teacher-training programs throughout the state could collaborate on how to help move public education into the 21st century.

The summit keynote address featured Dr. Thomas Carroll, president of the National Commission on Teaching and America's Future, who delivered the message: "You need to get out of the teacher training business and you need to do it fast. You need to get into the education development business, creating learning experts." Dr. Carroll's message, while startling at first, for the most part seems to have been well received, and an IHE network has been formed. The fact that, for the first time, these programs are formally and informally talking to each other about the subject of how to transform their programs is very significant. The IHEs have been fully informed and have provided input into the shaping of the revised rules for educator preparation. Through communicating and learning from one another, the likelihood of success in transforming higher education will be greatly improved.

Part III

The New Model for Learning

20th Century Versus 21st Century

6 Time Versus Mastery

Every educator knows and accepts that students have different learning styles and learn at different paces. So what is the logic of a time-based system in which students are required to show up at school buildings for fixed periods? Similarly, why should cohorts of students move forward by time-based grade levels? These time-based concepts are the steel in the framework of our educational systems. Yet the authors have concluded that rather than holding up the institution, they are causing it to fail. America needs a new model of public education.

TIME

The primary constant in America's system of public education is time. Generally speaking, it's 180 days; from August/September into May/June; from 7:30 a.m. until 3:30 p.m.; first, second, third, and fourth quarters; first grade, second grade, eighth grade, twelfth grade. We've established a system based on blocks of time. Does the logic of this 100+-year-old system hold up in 21st century America?

Let's begin with the message that we send to our students when we start the school year around the beginning of September and end it in May or June. Do we inadvertently communicate that learning begins at the start of the school year and ends at the end of it? We communicate that summer is not for learning, that is, unless you've done a bad job during the school year and have to endure summer school. We communicate that summer means fun and September means that the fun is over and now we need to start learning again. Is that the message that we should be sending?

With regard to the daily school schedule, if we communicate that the best time for learning is 7:30 a.m. to 3:00 p.m., we minimize the importance of the activities that students may participate in while not in school.

WHAT ABOUT SUMMER VACATION?

It may still be logical to consider the custodial nature of keeping elementary-aged children in a safe and supportive environment for periods of the day and year so that parents may feel secure about where their children are while they are at work or taking care of other functions of family life. But, even for elementary school children, is the 180-day, 7:30 a.m.-to-3:30 p.m. schedule the right schedule for either learning or family life?

For now, let's look at the 180-day schedule from a family-life perspective. While we know that parents, especially moms of elementary aged children, appreciate the opportunities that school gives them to take care of other aspects of their lives, their jobs and family functions don't stop in mid-June. It is likely that a significant percentage of parents would gladly take advantage of schooling opportunities made available longer into the summer, possibly even all year. Further, it is logical that the way a family would utilize school opportunities, if available all year long, would differ with each family and each child.

But that's not how school works. School sets the schedule and everybody must conform whether it works well or not. Would there be a demand for school if it were available all year long and could be accessed based on individual families and their children's needs? Our guess is that everyone says "yes." So why don't we do that? Any business would tell you that, if there were an untapped consumer need, a business capable of filling the need would probably do so. So then, why hasn't the void been filled?

In many ways, some less than optimal, the void has been filled. It has been filled by summer camps for families that can afford it. It has been filled by babysitters, by day care centers, and by not-for-profits like the Boys and Girls Clubs. It has been filled by home schooling and by online learning. Some of these options actually do a reasonable job of stimulating learning. Others are terrible. At worst, children who should not be left either unsupervised or poorly supervised are left with an older brother, sister, or ineffective babysitter who is ill equipped to ensure that positive things happen during that period. This is, in many ways, a money issue. Affordability is often the primary determinant of what happens with the children during these periods. The National Summer Learning Association reports that much of the learning that takes place during the school year is

lost over the summer by students from poor families; students from families who can afford positive options during summers retain a measurably
significant amount more of what they learned during the school year.
(Fairchild, Smink, & Steward, 2009).

It seems logical that public education would attempt to remedy this
problem. The building costs are pretty much the same. The added expense
is, primarily, personnel. Would this added cost be borne solely by the taxpayers? Not necessarily. There are other ways to address cost issues. After
all, the babysitters, Boys and Girls Clubs, and day care centers all have
costs associated with them, and those funds do not come from taxpayers.
Additionally, it is possible that the Boys and Girls Clubs and day care centers could work in conjunction with the public schools to help address this
issue of learning during the summer months. Couldn't the public system
provide assistance to these community-based entities to ensure that high-
quality learning experiences will take place there not just during the
summer but all year long?

THE CARNEGIE UNIT

At the turn of the 20th century, the Carnegie Unit became widely used as
a measure of the amount of time a high school student participated in an
academic subject. As high school education was becoming more commonplace, there needed to be a standard measure for admission to higher education. The unit was defined as a total number of hours of study in a high
school course meeting multiple times in a week. This usually equates to
120 to 150 hours or approximately 45 minutes per day per course in a
180-day school year. It was generally held that 14 Carnegie Units in academic subjects represented the preparation needed for higher learning.

As the Carnegie Unit became standardized into systems of learning,
the credit-bearing course structure of high school took hold nationally.
Since its inception, the normed culture for learning at the high school level
has been that when a student meets the criteria for seat time and passes the
course with whatever passing grade is defined by the school, that credit is
then earned.

This 20th century model for learning at the secondary level still has a
vise-like grip on learning early in the 21st century. When probing why
there is such reluctance to move away from it, secondary educators generally stay fixed on the Carnegie Unit as being the only acceptable criterion
for college admission and, therefore, immutable. In reality, colleges admit
students from International Baccalaureate programs, portfolio-based high
schools, charter schools, virtual high schools, and home schools. It is

becoming increasingly difficult to fit these learning experiences into a Carnegie Unit model for acquiring credit.

The 21st century model for learning is, in a sense, also based on time—not seat time, but a different amount of time for every student. Students learn at different rates based on learning style, learning preference, and readiness for learning a particular content area. Students hybridize learning with online learning opportunities as well as real-world learning opportunities, oftentimes learning independently or with multiple teachers and educators involved in assessing student learning. Increasingly, colleges are instituting experiential learning programs as part of undergraduate studies. Southern New Hampshire University is now offering College Unbound, a completely experiential-learning undergraduate degree designed for the student who prefers to learn differently.

PLACE

Another constant from the old system is place: school buildings. As mentioned previously, a logical possibility may be to have the public system assist not-for-profit organizations to become true places of learning all year long. Some might argue that this would siphon off students from school buildings and reduce the need of the public system's facilities. Another perspective is it might be more cost effective to use the facilities of not-for-profit organizations more regularly than they have traditionally been used, that it would increase their community importance for the children they serve, and that they could even be upgraded to serve their newly elevated function for less than what the public system currently spends.

"If I could show you how to make a quality education available year round by providing more learning opportunities for kids than ever before, without costing more money, would you be interested?" Perhaps this is an offer that we should not refuse. The goal becomes to use the public system to strengthen the learning capacities of the public library, the preschools, the day care centers, the museums, the arts centers, the fitness centers, the science centers, and our businesses. In the process, these existing institutions are transformed into even more valuable community assets that become vital components of how students learn. When students learn what the school thinks that they should learn, regardless of where and how they learn, should that learning count in the eyes of the public system? We've surveyed this time and time again with audiences of educators using whiteboards and remote-control responders. While virtually every time we've tried this, the vast majority says "yes," almost always, there are one or two in the audience who vote "no." This is a phenomenon, because when we've asked the same questions without use of the technology and simply called for a show of hands, there's never a "no" in the audience. Perhaps the anonymity of the remote controls gives the skeptics the courage to say "no."

So why would anyone say that school needs to be 180 days and that learning needs to take place inside the walls of the school? It is possible that they see this as inevitably leading to the deconstruction of the public school system as we know it and that they don't want the system to dramatically change. It could be because they believe that the system is generally fine the way it is and, therefore, it should be left intact. It could also be for more personal reasons, seeing that this approach has the potential to fundamentally change their jobs. They may fear that the jobs of the future system are ones that they haven't been trained for or may not like. Despite the strong arguments in favor of this brand of reform, the change may seem too threatening or difficult to envision. While much of this may seem like conjecture to those who have not begun the process of transitioning to a new model of public education, these are the kinds of conversations taking place in New Hampshire. Once again, it will require skilled leadership to build trust in education faculties in order to move redesign forward in a collaborative effort.

> *Fred recalls: I love being in classrooms, interacting with students. What I didn't love, when I was a teacher, was being in the same classroom/place, five days a week, five periods a day. My sense is that having a variety of places where I could perform my duties, sometimes in a classroom, sometimes in the community, sometimes online, would be a more exciting and effective profession.*

ANYTIME, ANYPLACE, ANYHOW, ANY PACE

The alternative to a time-based system that takes place inside of school buildings can be described as *anytime, anyplace, anyhow, and at any pace*. Ultimately, we advocate year-round learning. Year-round learning does not mean that students will be inside of schools all year long. Rather, what it means is that school will not simply be a reference to a building but will refer to the process of learning; that process of learning needs to have no perceived starts and stops (i.e., September–June), especially in the eyes and minds of students.

Students must be reoriented in their notions about what school is, especially when and where learning occurs. They need to understand that valuable learning can occur anytime and any place and can happen in many different ways. They need to understand what is expected of them (i.e., mastery of required competencies), how they will be assessed, and the variety of avenues for acquiring those skills and lessons, in and outside of the school, as well as through online and blended learning approaches. Similarly, educators should be reoriented to their new and vital roles:

- to facilitate the process of learning anytime, anyplace, anyhow, and at any pace
- to motivate all students to dream and achieve beyond what they would have on their own
- to be formal advocates for their students in order to help them reach their long- and short-term goals

While the word *teach* was not mentioned in the above bullet points, that doesn't mean that there will no longer be a need for our educators to function as classroom teachers. Educators may or may not be "teaching," in a traditional sense, for all or part of their duties. If there is a demand for classroom teaching, classroom teaching will exist as one of the ways that students are able to acquire their skills and knowledge. We would envision that the demand for traditional classroom approaches will continuously wane for a decade or two and may or may not remain a significant factor in how students learn in the future as online and real-world opportunities become more prevalent.

STUCK IN THE PAST

So why do we have a uniform calendar that runs from August or September to June? Some argue that it is based on an agrarian calendar that made time available for children to work in the fields, afternoons, and during the summer growing season. Others argue that it's not a true agrarian calendar because an agrarian society would have greater needs in the spring and fall. Yet others claim that it was to spare students from being cooped up in hot school buildings during summer months. Regardless, the arguments don't hold up in today's world. The vast majority of students no longer work in fields, and air conditioning in cars and buildings, which was rare decades ago, is commonplace today.

We hold on to 180-day calendar for three primary reasons:

1. Tradition—Everybody understands and accepts that this is how the school calendar is structured. The entire community plans around it. Seasonal businesses count on available student labor during the summer. Families plan their vacations. We've always done it this

way. Come September, everybody gets geared up for going back to school. Students finish their summer jobs, camps, or vacations. Businesses run back-to-school sales. Schools and districts crank up the school buses, dust and decorate their classrooms, and, we would like to assume, the learning magically follows. The traditional school calendar works on many levels—except, of course, for doing a sufficient job of educating our students.

2. Teacher contracts—Teacher contracts, for the most part, are based on that 180-day schedule. Teachers are paid to work the days specified in their contract. Most of these contracts specify that if teachers are required to work extra time beyond the 180 days, they must be compensated for that time. With school budgets constrained and school boards looking to save money virtually any way they can, the idea of paying for a longer school year gets dismissed quickly. We propose some solutions to this dilemma in Chapter 16.

3. Lack of air conditioning—While air conditioning is commonplace in today's businesses and public buildings, it is not always a given in America's classrooms. "We don't air condition classrooms because students are on vacation during the summer." Or, "Kids are out of school for the summer because it's too hot in non–air-conditioned classrooms."

Are any of these reasons nonnegotiable, preventing us from even considering a different schedule? Although not nonnegotiable, moving away from a traditional school calendar is not easy.

Of the three reasons, probably the easiest to overcome is the lack of air conditioning. The primary objection to air conditioning is the cost of installation and the related fuel costs. While a competency-based model can provide sufficient justification of the benefits of this upgrade, including the cost benefits, it is not the purpose of this book to convince districts to install air conditioning. Although the authors accept that air-conditioned schools can increase in-school opportunities for learning, this book's primary premise is based on the fact that valid learning experiences can happen anywhere and, therefore, take no position on a districts' willingness to incur the expense.

Tradition, on the other hand, must be addressed. The inertia of this tradition goes back more than a century. In order to overcome the inertia of the traditional school calendar, a well-thought-out plan needs to be clearly articulated and accompanied by, in the words of Nellie Mae Education Foundation President Nicolas Donohue, "a conscious decision to create public demand for a new model."

Creating demand for a new model cannot be achieved without very compelling reasons to change. That new model, a mastery-of-competencies model, has many compelling reasons, including

1. Cost effectiveness—a move-on-when ready/mastery-of-competencies model has many cost-saving components that will be powerful shapers of decision making, including

    a. The opportunity for students to finish their high school requirements in less than 4 years

    b. The utilization of community resources at a cost below similar offerings inside of the schools

    c. Technology—the 24/7/365 availability of limitless content at low cost or no cost that does not require school buildings, classrooms, or teachers

    d. Reduced construction needs—with more and more learning outside of traditional classrooms, there will be a reduced need for new school building construction.

2. Family friendly—Families will see that their personal needs/ lifestyles can be better accommodated in an anytime/anyplace learning model. It will allow families to schedule vacations or address other family needs without concern for rigid attendance policies that accompany traditional school schedules.

3. A high-quality, customized learning experience for every student will be the ultimate driver of a community's decision to move away from the traditional calendar. If change leaders can convince parents that this new model for learning will not cost more money and will enhance the likelihood of a rewarding future for their children, parents will drive the decision to change.

SCARCE RESOURCES VERSUS MANAGING ABUNDANCE

For as long as any of us have been alive, we've viewed the resources available in our public schools to be less than optimal. We have all heard the stories of teachers spending their own money to provide materials for their students. Teachers have complained for decades about the scarcity of resources.

So imagine if we look at this issue of resources totally differently. What if we looked at all of the resources available in our communities in order to harness them and make them available for our students? We can put a conscious effort into harnessing our arts assets, our fitness assets, and our science assets, all for the purpose of making them available to our students. We can seek out our nonprofit organizations, our business community, our public officials, retired scientists, and artists, recognizing that they can provide an abundance of resources for our learning mission. In so doing, we can transform the thinking of our educators' role from one of overseeing scarce resources to one of managing abundance. Managing abundance!

> *Fred recalls: I was first told of this notion of managing abundance by former New Hampshire Teacher of the Year and Principal of the Monadnock Community Connections School Kim Carter. Immediately, I got it and loved the concept.*

We've never thought of schools having abundance. But the abundance exists right outside of our walls and is available to us if we engage our communities in the conversation.

Student's Timetable

Any pace. As we transition to a move-on-when-ready/competency-based model, traditional K–12 grade levels will begin to disappear. When high school students understand that nights, weekends, and summers can now be a part of their formal learning and that traditional school attendance is no longer a mandated part of their educational experience, when they realize that they will only receive credit upon a demonstration of mastery of competencies, they will change their perspectives on their own learning. If students are aware that they can complete what was the equivalent learning of the traditional twelve grades in fewer years but can choose to remain in their school communities with their friends, to participate in seasonal sports, theater, and so forth while aggressively pursuing higher-level "courses" and possibly acquiring plus or minus 2 years of college before leaving high school, not only will students have real interest, but their parents, envisioning the better part of 2 years of college tuition going away, will become ardent advocates for this new model. This is an "everybody wins" model. Students win, parents win, taxpayers win, community organizations and businesses win, and educators win. Learning, when not constrained by artificial and arbitrary grade levels based on chronological age, will progress through a continuum that is documented along the way for the student, educators, and parents to continually review and plan forward.

What about those educators who don't successfully transition to this new model, who want things left as they were? Unfortunately (or, in some eyes, fortunately), educators clinging to an outdated model are at risk of becoming casualties of a competency-based system. This new model dictates that there needs to be a student-driven demand for every educator's services. As long as students perceive these teachers as individuals who relate well to students, who care about their future, and who will passionately advocate for them, there will likely be a demand for their services. If, however, that demand is not there, in all likelihood, their jobs will not be there either.

The good news for educators is that a 21st century, anytime, anyplace, anyhow, any pace, student-centered, move-on-when-ready model will rekindle the idealism that inspired most educators to enter the profession in the first place. Much of the frustrating nature of being in a static classroom environment, attempting to move a group of individuals along at a similar pace, classroom management issues, and the like will dissipate with this new system. Educators will play a more important role in students' lives and experience greater personal rewards, causing the primal juices that brought them to this profession to flow faster than ever. Their creativity, allowed near limitless freedom, will be unleashed for the benefit of students.

Instead of trying to advance the learning of approximately 20 students with a prescribed curriculum, this new model will call for a personalized/customized learning plan for each student. No two plans will look exactly alike. The results of this will be that students will march toward mastery of competencies at different paces. With this flexibility and freedom, student gains will not be limited by the progress of other students. If a student is capable of more than 1 year's growth in 1 year, after he or she has mastered required competencies, he or she will move to the next level. For example, the Core Competencies in math and language arts, while articulated in terms of "Grade 1, Grade 4," will be actualized into "Level 1, Level 4," allowing students to move to the next level when they have demonstrated mastery of the prior level. With the ability to demonstrate learning on a year-round basis, students will have more available time on task, resulting in larger numbers advancing more than 1 year/level in one year's time.

When allowed ownership of what they learn and when they learn and how they learn, advances beyond the traditional gains of the old model will be commonplace. While gains will be commonplace, how students get there and where they actually get to will vary. Some 6-year-old students (Grade 1/Level 1) will be able to master 8-year-old (Grade 3/Level 3) work in math while remaining at Grade 1/Level 1 in language arts. Regardless, they will move at their own pace, not one based on how others at their age level perform.

7 Competency-Based Learning

The 20th century model used the Carnegie Unit as a measure of learning. The 21st century model uses competency as a measure of learning. We define competency as a student's ability to transfer content and skill in and/or across content areas.

Competency-based learning asks students to learn important content information and skills. It also requires that a student demonstrate that learning by applying the content and skills in unique ways. Rather than assume that the magic number of hours defined by the Carnegie Unit yields true understanding, we should be identifying the learning competencies, benchmarking what mastery of those competencies looks like, and moving our students to mastery in a continuum that is not time dependent.

The Carnegie Unit has been used in both junior high and senior high models of education. In abandoning this seat-time approach, imagine if our K–12 system of learning used mastery of competencies as a measure of moving forward in learning.

Imagine Jessica, a 7-year-old student, opening the door of her school. By the time she is 7 years old, we already have a wealth of information about her family, her developmental historical information, her learning style, her readiness in literacy and numeracy, and her interests. As Jessica moves through her learning, this information will continue to build and be readily accessible to her learning team members. Jessica is a very able reader as she enters school, but her numeracy skills are not as strong.

Once inside her school environment, she will participate in many developmental activities with her peers, establishing a community of learners on a regular basis. Yet when it is time for her to move to her literacy block, she will access learning resources at her instructional level that will move her forward in her proficiency, at her own pace—not one prescribed by a curriculum program. This literacy learning may be coupled with skills-based learning in reading and writing as well as interdisciplinary learning in which she is applying her literacy skills in a variety of settings. Jessica, in fact, may move more quickly through some parts of her literacy learning, while sometimes she may get stuck for a while. During these difficult times, she may have to learn a particular topic differently in order to master the competencies defined in literacy. Jessica's school would have some activities that are associated with developmentally appropriate groups of children participating in them, while her learning activities will be with groups of learners at her readiness level. Rich assessment along the way would see Jessica moving through her learning at her pace while guaranteeing there are no gaps. She will be able to rely on her prior learning to master new material because she was required to master her competencies before moving on to new learning. Technology will play an integral role in Jessica's learning both in school and out of school. In fact, it won't really matter whether she has learned inside the school building, in a community setting at a summer camp, at home with her parents, or virtually online. Achieving mastery of the defined literacy competencies will drive her learning.

Although students will not move through grade levels based on a school year, levels of learning with defined competencies are at the core of school and state declarations for requirements for graduation. At upper levels of learning, the system is also based on competencies. Imagine Matt, a 14-year-old student who has demonstrated mastery of core competencies required for secondary learning. He is about to make some choices on what his next level of learning will look like. Matt and his parents will decide which studies will be in a classroom setting, which areas he will be learning solely online or in hybridized format, and the number of years he would like to take to master the required competencies for graduation. Matt is a very talented artist who mastered his lower-level visual arts competencies early on, so his program will probably include learning opportunities at the postsecondary level as part of his program. His transcript for postsecondary college admission will reflect grades he has received on his competency-based learning, an online portfolio of his artwork, as well as documentation of other dimensions of his learning such as responsibility, effort, and citizenship. His transcript may or may not record *where* he demonstrated competency—in an extended learning opportunity, online, or in a classroom. Credits for graduation would be earned through a documentation of mastery of competencies required for graduation, regardless of the pace Matt set for completing all of his competencies required for graduation.

In the 20th century model of education, instruction drives learning. Complex systems of content standards provide the backbone around which grade-level expectations for learning are defined. These expectations are then assessed on many different levels—classroom, grade, state, and national levels. This system of taking standards into the classroom drives the pace of 20th century instruction. Teachers take on these standards with the goal of teaching to curriculum completion within the school calendar.

> Competency is a student's ability to *transfer* content and skill in and/or across content areas.

Imagine what would happen if we just reversed the process. Standards are good things! The development of the National Common Core Standards in Language Arts and Mathematics is a step forward in reducing the impossible number of standards around which learning should be designed. Core standards in these disciplines, as well as all disciplines, are the evolutionary step needed to transform the current state of standards-based learning. If core standards truly are essential learning, then each student must learn them. The 20th century model rests on teachers guaranteeing that they have covered or taught hundreds of standards. In the 21st century model, learning is the driver, facilitated by educators. The core standards are the essential prioritized learning of which each student must demonstrate mastery before moving on to other essential learning. In the 21st century, the learner drives the learning.

STANDARDS VERSUS COMPETENCIES

What is the difference between a standard and a competency? Simply, standards are the *what* in learning, while a competency is the *why* of the learning. To illustrate the difference, imagine studying a unit of history about the Revolutionary War. Most fifth graders begin their appreciation for U.S. history as they study the birth of our nation. A competency for this unit would be: the student will understand that conflict and cooperation during the Revolutionary War shaped our government today. This goes far beyond the battles, locations, and historical figures. Students will study the war in the context of today's government. When these students move on to study the Civil War, they can connect with their previous understanding of the Revolutionary War to understand how conflict and cooperation further shaped our country today while connecting back to the conceptual learning of the Revolutionary War. A competency is synonymous to the enduring understanding that Wiggins and McTighe (2005) have eloquently framed in the *Understanding by Design* model in Stage 1 of unit design. In this stage of design, the declaration of the content and skills is also addressed. It is at this stage in unit design that a teacher will list all of the state and local standards pertinent to the unit. After the declaration of standards, it is very difficult to take the next, far more challenging step in design—that is, to delineate the "must know and be able to do" standards. Many teachers feel compelled to teach it all because each standard is state mandated. Thus the "breadth over depth" problem arises. Moving to essential learnings based on core standards in each discipline will go far in giving educators forgiveness to prioritize the content and skills found in units.

Sample competencies for United States history course:

1. Students will understand that conflict and cooperation together shape the development of the United States.

2. Students will understand that there is a relationship between civic ideals and practices.

3. Students will understand that in the history of the United States, the people and the environment impact each other.

4. Students will understand that decisions by individuals have driven forms of production, distribution, and consumption of goods and services over time.

5. Students will understand that as various cultures interact or collide on the American continent, each culture is impacted.

John Bransford (Bransford et al., 1999) speaks of expertise as the depth of learning that allows one to uniquely problem solve, while Wiggins and McTighe speak of enduring understandings as the learning that the student brings forward into future learning. Both expertise and enduring understanding go far beyond the discreet, atomistic nature of content and skills, or standards.

One is competent when one can demonstrate the ability to transfer content and skills in a unique situation. The ability to do so is the expertise that one brings to a situation. Some transfer of content and skills is direct, whereas some situations require more complex thinking. The important consideration here is not that a student knows it and can do it but that the student can show that he/she can then teach it to others and can transfer the learning in unknown situations.

When a teen embarks in learning how to drive, she engages in classroom learning of the laws and rules of the road. Her driving teacher has her practice the basic maneuvers of driving safely, and she then practices for a period of time with her parents or other licensed adults supervising her decision making until she is ready to take the test. On the day of her driving test, she will take both a written test to confirm her basic knowledge and then a practical test to demonstrate her driving skills. She will have to transfer everything she has learned about the driving laws and her experiences driving with her instructor and parents. Her demonstration of what she learned from practical experience built on core knowledge and skills represents her competency level. If she fails either the written or the practical tests of driving, she fails. If she passes, she has demonstrated her knowledge of the law, the skill set of handling a car, and her ability to make decisions while driving. She is competent! She has met mastery of the competencies required to deserve her (beginner's) driver's license. Yet this mastery would represent minimum competency. She will gain greater competency and mastery over time as she practices her skill set in new situations.

The conventional way we look at our learners is that they either know something or they don't. Using the lens of expertise, we can see that developing expertise is building on previous learning over time with multiple experiences in which to transfer learning along the way. Our teen driver is developing greater expertise in driving over time. In this same way, John Bransford (Bransford et al., 1999) speaks of developing expertise in students through their learning experiences. In effect, we need to look at our learners as somewhere on the continuum of novice to expert.

So too must we raise our standards-based teaching to the level of competency-based learning. It isn't enough for teachers to teach the standards. It is more important for the students to demonstrate what they have learned by applying their learning of those standards in real-life learning situations or engaging scenarios. This opens the schoolhouse door to learning that can take place anywhere and at a learner's pace. The architecture of curriculum development when designing competency-based learning is distinctly different than the process of teaching to the standards; in our 21st century model, students must build a firm foundation of essential learning on which to build future learning as well as demonstrate their level of mastery through high-quality performance tasks or applications of that learning.

MASTERY

The primary variable in public education is achievement. America's educational system is not designed to bring students to mastery. It is designed with time-based starts and stops, and, at the end of each stop, each student is judged to date by the acquisition of knowledge based, in large part, on some combination of subjective factors that varies from teacher to teacher. Effort, motivation, homework completion, and attendance may be powerful influencers in how a teacher grades a student. In the end, the grade is generally interpreted in many different ways by parents, students, teachers, and the community.

A mastery-based system is very different. In a mastery-based system, formative tasks are tools the teacher designs for the student to acquire learning. A summative assessment proves that the student has mastered the required competencies. When the student achieves mastery, he or she is done and well prepared to move to the next level of work.

So why will a poor student in a time-based system become an excellent student in a mastery-based system, especially if he or she is required to learn, basically, the same lessons and skills? Remarkable differences in results can be produced if that student has the opportunity to acquire the same skills, but on his/her timetable in his/her setting and in a way that is exciting and relevant.

For example, consider learning engineering in a classroom versus with inventor Dean Kamen's FIRST Robotics. To a student, one might be a boring classroom with complicated math and some uninteresting engineering types of tasks, while the other, the Robotics program, may seem like a fight, a battle of robots, a competition where audiences cheer and where the future engineers are the stars.

Rose: The difference between the traditional internship and an extended learning opportunity is that the student engages in a different relationship with the community-based organization. Traditionally, internships are based on a time-based system of earning credit—that is, "x" number of hours of on site attendance yields a credit. In an extended learning opportunity, a student engages in a learning experience that is competency based, exploring an essential question or probe designed by the student. The exploration of that probe through the learning experience requires the student to acquire content and skills in a particular discipline and apply them in the learning experience. Often, as a result of this learning opportunity, the student is able to share a product of his/her experience such that the organization can continue to benefit from it after the extended learning opportunity is over.

Yet we rarely marry these rich learning experiences to competencies connected to learning expectations that would propel students forward. These experiences are generally relegated to the "enrichment" experience. Kaylee Oberlies, a sophomore at Manchester Memorial High School, did a presentation on extended learning opportunities (ELOs) to the New Hampshire State Board of Education (Oberlies, 2011). Kaylee won the Francis Wayland Parker Award for her essay promoting more ELOs, especially to lower-income students. Based on her experience at Memorial, witnessing first hand the impact that ELOs were having on her fellow students, Kaylee stated, "The ultimate goal of [more ELOs] would be a dramatic decline in students suffering from bullying, distress, and depression" (Oberlies, 2011).

Table 1 Extended Learning Opportunity Examples

Samples of Credit-Yielding, Competency-Based Extended Learning Opportunities
Environmental science: In conjunction with a local environmental center, several students engaged in a forestry project with the forester, a wildlife survey, and a community garden project.
Pharmacology: Studying medications used in nursing homes and the study of hospital-based pharmacology
Poetry slam: Various poetry genres were explored in preparation for final student performances of original poetry at Manchester's Bridge Cafe, a nationally known poetry slam center—all filmed for peer and team review.
Media: Public television engaged several dozen students in television production, building competencies in videotaping, Final Cut Pro editing software, and concept creation as small teams of students produced dozens of independent short features, interviews, and comedies that looped on Manchester Public Television for months.
Humanities: Sited at St. Anselm's College, students developed project-management, presentation, technology, and computer software skills for 45 "new American" students who researched and exhibited multimedia presentations highlighting modern heroes in immigration. Each high school student was paired with college students and staff.
Fire science: At the Dover Fire Science Academy, students study firefighting with the Dover (NH) Fire Department and are able to complete Firefighter I certification and emergency medical technician training.
Biotechnology: Standardizing a lab procedure in cooperation with a college

When we allow students to own their learning, we can now ask each student to achieve mastery. "Mastery for virtually every student" may sound like an audacious goal, but it is attainable. "Isn't that too high a bar?" Not if time is no longer a barrier and students get to take true ownership of how, when, and where they will acquire the necessary skills; mastery is possible for virtually every student.

So, what is mastery? Does mastery in engineering mean rocket scientist level? Does mastery in music mean a virtuoso? Does mastery in French mean the skills of an interpreter? No. The word *mastery* must be accompanied by *of required competencies*. Mastery is an advanced level of proficiency in a learner's ability to apply skills and knowledge. For example, if the applications of basic addition, subtraction, multiplication, and division are required competencies for a particular math course, a student should not receive credit for mastering two or three out of four. The student should receive credit or move on when he/she has mastered all of the required competencies.

> Mastery is an advanced level of proficiency in a learner's ability to apply skills and knowledge.

Is passing a test proof of mastery? Maybe. Maybe not. That really depends on the validity of the test. If this assessment can only prove that a student has memorized formulas well enough to pass a scheduled test but will likely forget a significant portion of the information within a few weeks, it doesn't reveal proof of mastery. The more appropriate questions to ask are: Does the student's performance prove that the student really understands this material well beyond the test? And most importantly, is the student able to apply that learning in a variety of unknown situations in the future?

Mastery is not about a virtuoso level of skills, but, rather, the student clearly demonstrates the required competencies as defined by the course or unit of learning in the content area. As students continue to take on more challenging work, the required competencies that must be mastered may be at a virtuoso level.

In our earlier driver's test example, while the student has mastered the basic competencies to pass her driver's test, this does not grant her the license to drive a motorcycle, a tractor-trailer, a bulldozer, or any other vehicle for which mastery of a more complex level of competencies is required before a license is granted. While her initial driver's license may provide a foundational experience on which to build, a new set of related but different competencies must now be mastered.

Requiring mastery of our learners before moving on is the critical element of building systems of learning based on student assets instead of student deficits. Requiring mastery has a wonderful side effect: The student will be able to depend on that learning in future learning experiences. In our 20th century deficit model, we move students on in spite of the fact that they have demonstrated a lack of mastery. Without mastery, a learner cannot use that knowledge or skill in future learning. The cycle of disappointing results continues over and over again. Ask a high school math teacher about her students' mastery of fractions. Should we even be learning fractions at any level in high school mathematics? Probably not, but high school math teachers will tell you that many students never mastered it in elementary school. Why would we ever think that students will get it on their own after demonstrating failure in third grade?

DOCUMENTING MASTERY

How do we document mastery? Thomas Guskey, Robert Marzano, Ken O'Connor, and Rick Wormeli (Guskey, 2008; Marzano, 2006; O'Connor, 2009; Wormeli, 2006) have eloquently put forth recommendations for grading practices that must be considered when communicating student learning. The teacher-to-teacher variability in arriving at a grade has contributed to the misunderstanding of what a grade should and does mean. Clearly, the traditional report card representing one grade for each subject matter, based on variable grading practices, falls short of adequately representing all aspects of student learning that should be communicated to parents and, ultimately, to institutes of higher education and the workplace.

In a competency-based learning environment, the achievement of a competency is communicated on an ongoing basis. Aspects of student performance such as attendance, effort, motivation, student professionalism, and cross-cutting skills (problem solving, critical thinking, etc.) should also be communicated on an ongoing basis but not as part of the achievement grade. Since mastery represents an advanced level of proficiency in content and skills whereby a student can transfer learning in unique situations, high-quality assessment systems must be built into the learning. In keeping with the practices found in standards-based grading systems, the grade achieved in competency-based learning should be highly dependent on summative, evaluative assessments. These summative assessments should be multiple and varied in format. The evaluative criteria for these summative assessments should include performance tasks as well as written tasks. Formative assessment (practice, checks for understanding, probes for knowledge and skills gained) along the learning path, which is not evaluative, should not be considered in the competency-based grade. Formative assessments are of great value for both the student and the teacher in the learning pathway. Furthermore, competency in any given area may be gained over time. Therefore, the averaging of a grade over time does not adequately represent the level of mastery of the competency. Use of rolling grades or an achievement grade determined by trending of grades earned is more accurate in communicating the level of mastery of a competency.

What is that magic grade that represents mastery? Most high schools grant credit for high school courses with an earned grade of 60, 65, or 70. When we ask educators if these are "magic numbers" that represents mastery, they invariably tell us no. But, if high schools grant credit for such an earned grade, they are, in essence, declaring 60, 65, or 70 as mastery. At the elementary level, students are moved forward in their learning in spite of a declaration that a student has not met the standard. We have settled for mediocrity in our systems of learning when we have allowed students to move on with insufficient achievement as represented in their grades.

In bringing students to a mastery of competencies, relearning and reassessment emerge as necessities rather than options. This is a practice that is currently more common at the elementary level than at the secondary level where, generally, the student's grade on the test is the prime motivator for a student to request a retake. In a competency-based classroom, rich formative assessment paves the way for learners to be prepared for the summative or performance assessment.

At several New Hampshire high schools, when a student does not demonstrate mastery, a relearning and reassessment plan is designed. The student writes reflectively on the reasons for the poor performance on the assessment and then goes on to propose steps to relearn. If the student honestly reflects that he/she did not put an honest effort in completing work or studying to the degree necessary, the relearning plan is designed around that component of relearning. If the student declares that it was a concept in learning that remained a mystery to him/her, a different type of relearning may be suggested. Once the teacher reviews the plan, it is signed by both teacher and student and then signed by the parent. Only after the relearning plan is complete is the reassessment taken. Only the parts of the first assessment that were weak or not learned are assessed the second time around.

Relearning/Reassessment Plan

Student Name: _____ Date: _____

Title of Assessment: _____

To the student: Review the attached assessment. It is important for you to reflect and understand the reasons for the grade you received on this assessment. It is also important that you use this knowledge to design a plan that results in a successful reassessment.

1. Review the attached assessment. List the content areas or topics that you feel you will need to relearn or study:

_____

_____

_____

_____

2. List the reasons you performed poorly on these topics:

_____

_____

_____

_____

3. Design a plan that will lead you to a successful reassessment.

_____

_____

_____

_____

Upon successful completion of your reassessment plan, a time and format for the reassessment will be determined.

Student signature: _____

Teacher signature: _____

Parent signature: _____

Going from traditional grading practices to competency-based grading practices, which allow open reassessment, is a huge paradigm shift for most teachers. Introducing this practice incrementally over time has allowed for the change in professional practice as well as the change in learning culture for students. As a result of this practice, learners become secure in the content knowledge and skills they will need for future learning, and they are more successful. When relearning and reassessment lead to successful students, the need for credit recovery is reduced. When grading is tracked by competency, students who fail a competency need only address relearning and demonstrate mastery of that competency rather than spend weeks in the summer in generalized learning.

Spaulding High School in Rochester, New Hampshire, has a unique grading system. Grades at Spaulding are communicated to parents and students as A, B, C, NYC, or IWS. A rubric is used to describe each grade. NYC indicates "not yet competent." If a student receives NYC for a grade, the student then goes into a relearning and reassessment plan for the course competencies that he/she has not yet mastered. The relearning may be targeted work with a teacher coach, an extended learning opportunity to target competency, or a virtual learning opportunity. IWS indicates "insufficient work submitted." When a student receives an IWS for a grade, it means that the teacher is unable to determine that student's mastery level. In this event, the student would then go into some form of credit recovery such as a virtual learning opportunity, an extended learning opportunity, or a retake of the course. Rethinking and redesigning learning time, as part of a master schedule for the purpose of relearning at the secondary level, is a challenge. Yet it is a major landmark in transforming school practices.

In a competency-based learning environment, learners are brought to mastery through just-in-time learning of content and skills over a period of time. Relearning and reassessment are integral to bringing students to mastery. Again, when we engage educators in a discussion as to what grade represents mastery, few defend keeping the current, traditional grading system. However, moving parents and students to new thinking about grades representing achievement of competency requires a change of teacher practices and the culture for grading in our schools.

When New Hampshire high schools were required to grant credit based on student mastery of competencies, the failure of the traditional grading system became apparent quickly. One high school used traditional grading but based summer school on passing course competencies. Parents were outraged that their students earned As and Bs on their report cards yet had to report to summer school to pass a competency. The inadequacy of traditional grading brought many schools to standardize the

Competency to Grading Framework

Competency
- "Students will understand that . . ."
- "Students will demonstrate the ability to . . ." (described at Levels 3 or 4 on Webb's Depth of Knowledge)

Performance Indicators
- "I can . . . " statements reflecting transfer of content and skills at Levels 1, 2, 3/4 of Webb's Depth of Knowledge

Grading
- Summative Assessments: grades on Performance Indicators at Level 3/4 on Webb's Depth of Knowledge
  ○ Weighting: 90% or more of final grade
- Formative Assessments: checks for learning along the way, mostly tracked rather than graded
  ○ Weighting: 10% or less of final grade

grading practices: no zeros, 90% or more of a grade dependent on summative assessments, relearning/reassessment plans, and the recording of assessments by competency rather than format of assessment (test, quiz, project). Competency-based grade reform in high schools has been the driver of change in assessment and instruction. It has brought high school teachers to reflect on the need for fair grading practices. Several schools have created grading philosophy statements to guide teacher practices. Ongoing work in moving summative assessment from paper-and-pencil format to problem-/project-based performance assessment has been a natural evolution when teachers strive to determine if a student has met mastery of a competency. Performance indicators require teachers to design learning tasks and assessments tuned to Webb's Depth of Knowledge, a four-tiered taxonomy of task complexity. Competency, by its definition, requires strategic and extended thinking; thus, learning tasks and performance indicators must be designed in the learning pathway. Sample grading philosophy statements and a competency-based report card are found in the Resources section of this book.

8 Learning in the 21st Century

If we were basing everything specifically on time, we'd conclude that we are now more than 10% into the 21st century. But we don't always interpret our world according to such precise measurements. At the first New Hampshire Summit on Developing 21st Century Educators (May 2010), keynote speaker Dr. Tom Carroll, President of the National Commission on Teaching and America's Future (NCTAF), spoke of how Americans classify '50s and '60s music (Carroll, 2010). He stated that we don't necessarily think of '50s music as having been created in a precise timeframe of the music between 1950 and 1959 or '60s music as the music between 1960 and 1969.

Those of us who follow popular music trends think of '50s music as starting with the birth of rock 'n roll, which began, arguably, with Elvis Presley's "That's All Right, Mama" in 1954 or Bill Haley & His Comets' "Rock Around the Clock" in 1955. Additionally, we don't see '50s music ending in 1959. In the early '60s, many '50s doo-wop groups were still cranking out hits, as were other early rock 'n roll pioneers. To validate this, simply turn on your Sirius or XM radio to the '50s and '60s stations, and you will hear Sam Cooke's "Chain Gang" (1960), Dion's "Runaround Sue" (1961), the Four Seasons' "Sherry" (1962), and the Kingsmen's "Louie, Louie" (1962)—all played on the '50s channel. The American musical soundscape changed with the British Invasion (the Beatles, Rolling Stones, Yardbirds, etc.). But that didn't start until late 1963 and really hit hard in 1964. So what we refer to as '60s music didn't really start until about 1964.

Tom Carroll applied similar reasoning to current American educational practice when he went on to talk about how, educationally speaking, we are not in the 21st century. He talked about how the cornerstone of the 20th century model is a stand-alone teacher in a classroom. To emphasize his point, he displayed photographs in his PowerPoint of a stand-alone teacher in a classroom from the 1950s and a stand-alone teacher in a classroom from today (Carroll, 2010). In most of America's schools, we are still stuck in this 20th century model. Tom Carroll states: "The 21st century will begin when we abandon schools dedicated to the delivery of text-based, graded instruction in stand-alone classrooms. We're not in the 21st century yet in education. Does this mean that traditional, stand-alone teachers in classrooms don't have a place in the 21st century? Most likely they will, especially in early childhood education; but the stand-alone teacher in a classroom, especially at the secondary level, will not likely be the dominant model for the 21st century" (New Hampshire Department of Education, 2010).

In the 21st century, much of school will begin to look like the real world because much learning will be in real-world settings. In the 21st century, much of school will be based on technology, not as a visual aid for a teacher in a classroom, but more like the Internet is being used for learning today. Online courses will continue to improve and play an increasingly significant role in how learning happens for our students. Will traditional classrooms still be a measurable part of the 21st century in education? Yes, but only the best will survive and, as the century progresses, we anticipate significant reductions in the number of traditional classroom experiences as we get deeper into the 21st century.

While this may sound to some like nice theory, the experiences in New Hampshire and other parts of the country, like Cooperative Education Service Agency #1 (CESA #1) in Wisconsin, will clearly demonstrate that the 21st century education model is beginning to emerge.

USING THE RIGHT PERSPECTIVE

No Child Left Behind ushered in an era of intense data warehousing and data analysis. As schools and school districts were increasingly being placed on the School or District in Need of Improvement (SINI or DINI) list within their states, schools turned inward to analyze the implications of the state assessment results. School data teams became more proficient in the statistical language of the tests. School systems developed benchmark assessments across grade levels in schools within a district so that one school could be compared to another and groups of students could be compared to other groups of students.

Generally, data are analyzed to uncover student weaknesses, with a resulting action to address the weakness with some form of reteaching. This can take many different forms, mostly at the elementary level. Sometimes, a student is given more time to learn something that he or she missed first time through. Sometimes, students go to a smaller group to redo what they did the first time through. High schools generally have fewer resources or flexibility of schedule to build much reteaching into the school day. In the 20th century model, credit recovery by taking the whole course over can sometimes be the only recourse for many students who fail. Often, in spite of some additional relearning, the student may be moved on to the next topic under study because the teacher is moving forward with the curriculum.

Despite having access to vast collections of student data, we may not be warehousing and using student data that can have the greatest impact on learning. Learning style profiles, areas of student strengths and weaknesses, interest surveys, sports interests, cocurricular school activities, participation in community sports and organizations, family demographics, health and wellness information—all these factors that affect student learning generally are left out of the databases teachers use on a regular basis in crafting learning experiences for students.

In a 21st century learning environment, all of this information would continually be updated as a learner moves through school. Student strengths would be used to overcome weaknesses, while the data would be rich in information to assist a teacher in finding ways to connect with a learner at the beginning of the learning cycle or when the learner experiences a stumbling block.

More often than not, the less advantaged school districts are looking for any way possible to engage their students. These forward-thinking administrators embrace using students' strengths to conjure up exciting options that can be made available for their students as a positive change in how they go about the business of getting students to learn.

Fred recalls: Dr. Jean Richards, Superintendent of Schools of the Raymond, New Hampshire, School District, called and asked me if I would come in and speak to her school board, high school faculty, and the entire sophomore and junior classes at Raymond High School. The students were gathered in the multipurpose room, and I was introduced to them. I began my remarks by saying, "For the first time in your lives, we are going to have a conversation about rules and regulations that you are going to love."

There was clear skepticism on the faces of the students as I began my conversation with them. But, as they started to understand the direction and inherent flexibility and student-centered nature of New Hampshire's regulations, you could start to see eyes widen and minds fully engage . . . to the point of excitement.

(Continued)

(Continued)

One young lady raised her hand and said, "I hate math. I can't do it. I've never been able to do math, even when I was in kindergarten. How is it possible that there would be a way that I can learn math?"

I responded to her, "Tell me something that you love."

She enthusiastically said, "I love guitar."

I explained, "Do you understand that so much of the nature of music is based on mathematics? All of the notes are fractions. Each note on the fret board is based on a frequency of vibrations. It's all mathematically based. If I could show you how to learn to play guitar better by understanding the mathematics involved in making the sounds of your guitar, do you think you'd be interested in that?"

She said, "Yes."

The next student, a young man, raised his hand. He said, "It's not exactly music, but I do sound engineering for a band after school every day."

I responded, "Sound engineering is physics. Would you be interested in turning your sound engineering into a science credit?"

He said, "Yes."

Immediately, a teacher in the room called the student's name. It was his science teacher, who told the young man to come see him after school so they could figure out how to make his sound engineering count for credit toward graduation.

Later, after the assemblies were over, Dr. Richards and I were walking in the hallway. One of the students came up to us and said, "That was the best assembly we've ever had."

Dr. Richards smiled.

Where 20th century learning relies on analyzing data to remediate, 21st century learning relies on collecting and analyzing rich data while responding to the known learner needs, as well as strengths, to optimize student success along the way.

SILOS

Do you remember a time when learning was really fun? Do you remember going home excited at the end of the day to share what you learned that day? If you think back to those experiences, you may well be describing a wonderful experience you had in kindergarten. Think about it. What did it look like? Your teacher probably decided to pick a theme that would connect all the learning. Take apples, for example. Your teacher may have chosen to engage you in storybooks that featured apples. Through those wonderful storybooks, you learned the fundamentals of the English language. You probably ate apples for your snack that week. You also counted apples for your math lesson. You may also have visited an apple orchard to view your community's connection to farming. In other words, you experienced your learning connected through one theme.

As learners move upward through our system of learning, the connectedness and experiential nature of learning shifts. Elementary teachers who have experienced the one-room classroom of teaching multiple subjects in a day can relate how they could create learning experiences for children that were connected to each other while immersing the students in the learning. They would also relate that with the dawn of standardized testing and "canned" programs, they lost their versatility and creativity in designing engaging experiences that brought the worlds of language arts, math, social studies, and science together for their students.

Why did this happen? Standardized test results uncovered many gaps. In fact, many teachers, working in isolation, would design mega units that were steeped in engagement but lacking in a focus of the learning targets. In trying to align instruction to content, the rich interconnectedness of teaching became a matter of checking off standards that were incorporated within content-area teaching. Thus, curriculum silos grew taller and taller, especially with the prevalence of canned programs within curriculum areas adopted by school districts to improve test results. Elementary school began to look much like high school without the bells and movement from class to class. But students nonetheless moved from content to content, oftentimes without connecting their thinking and their learning from one area to another.

At the middle level, many schools organized themselves into interdisciplinary teams that shared common planning periods in order to connect the learning across curriculum areas. Just when such middle-level learning systems were breaking down the junior high school approach to content learning, standardized tests and standards alignment rang the death knell to many rich interdisciplinary units of inquiry and study for adolescent learners. It was back to the silos at the middle level.

This 20th century model of learning is based on an organization of content by discipline that is articulated over a 10- to 12-year period of time. Curriculum may be rigidly incorporated into programs of content study so that both teachers and students march together within a content area to a curriculum map that discreetly breaks down the content into parcels of content delivery across the school year. With the development of these curriculum silos, teachers feel the need to march through content, checking off standards, and hopefully making it to the end of the curriculum map before the school year ends.

The result of the curriculum silos, deeply entrenched in the scheduling of learning time in schools, has also pre-empted our ability to recognize and structure learning in ways in which we know how the human brain actually learns. John Medina in *Brain Rules* (Medina, 2009) notes that school would look very different if we paid attention to how the brain works. If we do pay attention, we would encourage frequent movement to oxygenate the brain, create social settings in which students interact in their learning, recognize that harmful stress situations impede learning, and recognize that, for some students, the time of day may play a major factor in the ability to learn well.

In addition to content silos, we also have the silos of curriculum, instruction, and assessment. There has been incredible research and findings in each of these areas of educational theory, but there has been very little crossover to break through the isolation of one area of educational theory to another.

Just as with the apples example, in the 21st century model, we would not expect our students to learn individual disciplines independently of one another. Educators having expertise in various disciplines would look at the body of knowledge and skills required of the learner at a given level. In a collaborative effort of planning for engaging learning, the educators would use their knowledge of their students' levels of mastery and their learning styles, preferences, and interests. The educators would work collaboratively to create rich inquiry-based learning that connects the content areas. Our 21st century learners will not be problem solving in silos but would be connecting abstract concepts from more than one discipline. In this new model, students would partner with teachers to solve a unique real-world problem presented at the beginning of the learning cycle. Each student would know how his or her learning was connected to the competencies of the learning and what criteria would be used to determine mastery of the competencies that the student would be called upon to demonstrate while learning along the way and at the conclusion of the learning cycles.

Rose: In creating the competency-development template in the C.A.C.E.S. model, teachers constructed engaging scenarios—complex learning tasks that engage students in learning. These scenarios became the assessment framework for the unit of study. Engaging scenarios are ideal for hooking students of any grade level or content area at the beginning of a unit of study. An example of an engaging scenario for a unit of study in ecology: you have been asked to serve as the chairperson of your lake's milfoil management committee. Milfoil is an exotic, invasive species in the lake. You will be making a presentation to the lake residents proposing that diver-assisted suction harvesting instead of herbicides be used to control milfoil. Residents should be informed about the effects milfoil has on lake ecology and the pros and cons of use of both suction harvesting and herbicide application.

The exploration of this real-world-learning problem would find the educators sometimes giving direct instruction to students just in time to apply that learning to the problem. Exploration and inquiry may cause the students to extend their learning in a community-based setting, virtually, or in a resource within the school environment. The dynamism of this model propels the learning from learning in the industrial-era model (classroom) into the 21st century (the real world). In this exploratory learning, the teacher provides the hook for the learning experience by crafting relevant learning opportunities. Direct just-in-time instruction is required for students to then apply the learning in the unique scenario. At that point in time, the teacher's role shifts to a more collaborative or coaching model.

The notion of facilitating learning or partnering with students in the learning process (Prensky, 2010) breaks down many of the imaginary walls we have created when driving standards or working in departmental disciplines. The content-area expertise is essential for the educator, but the practice of collaborating with educators to facilitate learning in cross-disciplinary opportunities serves the learner needs. Most real-world learning, which is of great relevance to learners, is rarely isolated to one discipline area.

Rose: In developing the extended learning opportunity plans, teachers consider the unique community-based learning opportunity while focusing on the learning outcomes of the experience. Rarely does such a rich learning experience involve one discipline alone. The axis between science, social studies, and English is a natural when a student is studying environmental science in a water-testing laboratory. The axis between math, English, and history is a natural one when a student is studying the geometry of stained glass while interning with an artisan. Working interdisciplinary learning into the fabric of a competency system of learning is essential in meeting the challenges of time and resources in designing learning systems.

9 Dropouts Versus Engaged Learners

"**Y**ou can pay me now or pay me later" was the line from the old Fram Oil Filter commercial, implying that it would have been cheaper to do the right thing earlier rather than failing to properly address the issue, resulting in a much larger problem later on. High school dropouts fit in this analogy. The proof exists in prisons all over America.

> *Fred recalls: As chairman of the State Board of Education, I asked for one of our monthly meetings to be held at the New Hampshire State Prison in Concord. The prison officials gave us the tour of the facilities, especially their educational facilities. They informed us that, at the time, 84.7% of the male population in New Hampshire's prisons did not have a high school diploma.*

TWO KINDS OF DROPOUTS

Former New Hampshire governor Craig Benson would often remark that there are two kinds of dropouts, the ones we count, who actually leave school, and then there are the psychological dropouts, the ones who have mentally checked out and are simply going through the motions because they know that they need a high school diploma. Governor Benson was one of those psychological dropouts. A high school guidance counselor told him that he "was not college material." In 1991, *Inc.* magazine named him National Entrepreneur of the Year.

Those comments from his guidance counselor left an indelible scar on his soul. In his inaugural address to the New Hampshire Legislature

(Benson, 2003), the governor passionately told that story and stated, "No longer are we going to allow the hopes and dreams of young people to be stomped on by the system." What a powerful statement. Is it true? Has the system done this to more than just a young Craig Benson? Are there many young people who, for whatever reason, weren't motivated to perform well within the system, that the system, frustrated, lashed out at with hurtful comments that have scarred kids for life? Is it possible that these comments actually caused real damage to the psychological makeup of some of these unengaged students; damage in real terms; damage that you can't see but you know is there, a loss in confidence and self-esteem; a bolstering of an inner fear that for some reason you aren't very smart and are not capable of achieving something special? How sad. Is this behavior on the part of educators common? Probably not, in the sense of the percentage of students in America's schools, but do these hurtful comments happen every day in schools across our country? Probably. Are these educators simply bad people, or is this just a symptom of a frustrated public school system that, as structured, is incapable of accomplishing the goal of engaging every student?

How much money do we have to pour into a system before we figure out that it's not yielding the kinds of results that we find acceptable? As most are aware, the system, as it exists, was never designed to successfully educate every student. It was designed to figure out which 25 to 30% of students were smart enough to go to college and to send the rest of the students on to the military or into the workforce, where factory jobs paid reasonable wages, allowing individuals the opportunity to own their piece of the American Dream, generally viewed at the time as a home, a family, a car or two in the driveway, and probably a dog. As the factory jobs went away, the need to ensure that every student was educated enough to be able to successfully find a place in our society became more and more important. The problem is that we are trying to accomplish this honorable goal in a system that was never designed to do so.

In order to truly engage each student, the 21st century system of education must be built from the ground up to address the whole child: the personal, social, physical, and academic needs of each student—not all students, each student. While this, to some, may sound like semantics, if someone is addressing all students, what is the level of assurance that all students are sufficiently engaged? When addressing each, the level of engagement becomes obvious and the changes necessary to ensure engagement are far clearer.

RACE TO ZERO

In 2003, the New Hampshire State Board of Education began moving its plan to revamp the state education regulations, promising greater flexibility than ever and promising students the opportunity to take a leadership role in their own education. At that time, the high school dropout rate in New Hampshire became a huge issue. The New Hampshire Center for Public Policy Studies had just issued a report called "One in Four," indicating that 25% of New Hampshire's students drop out of high school (Hall, 2003). While the New Hampshire Department of Education disagreed with the 25% figure, estimating that the number was more like 20%, the cries for lowering the dropout rate were everywhere.

Fred recalls: As chair of the board, I was making presentations on the proposed regulation changes virtually morning, noon, and night. I began incorporating in my presentations that if students are allowed to own what, when, where, and how they learn, why would anyone drop out of school? I would regularly add that we should not look at lowering the dropout rate; we should be looking at eliminating dropouts.

Occasionally, I would get pushback from those statements. At one event, a well-regarded superintendent suggested to me that I stop making those statements because eliminating dropouts was not possible. I responded that if we cling to the old system, I would agree, but we're going to go in a whole new direction and that "zero dropouts" was possible. He and I never agreed.

When the change in administrations occurred with the election of Governor John Lynch (2005) and subsequent replacements of both the commissioner and state board chairman, I backed off my rhetoric, not knowing whether a new direction would come with a new administration. When I realized that the new commissioner, Dr. Lyonel Tracy, was, for the most part, moving in the same direction as the draft standards, I would speak to Lyonel about eliminating dropouts.

On the morning of Governor Lynch's first statewide Dropout Summit (2005), Commissioner Tracy was the guest on New Hampshire Public Radio's (WEVO) The Exchange with host Laura Knoy. I listened as Lyonel stated that we shouldn't be looking at lowering the dropout rate; we should be looking to eliminate dropouts. I got very excited. Now our new commissioner was saying it.

At the summit, I approached Governor Lynch and told him that I had just heard Lyonel on WEVO say that we should eliminate dropouts. Within an hour, as Governor Lynch was making his remarks to the summit attendees, he stated that we should eliminate dropouts. This was the start of a public effort not to lower the dropout rate but to eliminate high school dropouts. Public statements were made by the governor, the commissioner, and the state board of education to eliminate dropouts in New Hampshire high schools by 2012. People now knew that we were serious.

Additionally, Governor Lynch campaigned for raising the age at which students were allowed to drop out of high school from 16 to 18 years. When the state board was asked to support this proposal, there was concern that, having been former Governor Craig Benson's state board chair who had been replaced by newly elected

(Continued)

(Continued)

Governor Lynch, I might come out against the proposal. The full state board, including me, endorsed the governor's proposal. At a subsequent event in Manchester, I saw Governor Lynch. He thanked me for supporting raising the dropout age. I said to him, "Governor, I'll tell you the same thing that I told the board: that if your proposal meant that, instead of boring students until they are 16, we will bore them until they are 18, it's not going to work. But we (the state board) have a plan. If students are allowed ownership of their learning, they won't drop out."

A number of school administrators voiced opposition to raising the age to 18 for fear that these students, who would have simply dropped out of school, would now remain in school being disruptive. When the law took effect, high schools had to reach out to the 16-year-olds who had dropped out to re-engage them with school until the age of 18. It was clear that many of these students could not re-enter school following the same program that they had disengaged from earlier. Because of the flexibility in the new regulations, re-engaged youth could choose from many different pathways to complete their programs. In effect, the new regulations are working and have become an accepted component of how school is delivered in New Hampshire. Students now know that if they want to get out of high school early, they can't simply kill time until they are 16. But if they do want to get out of school, for whatever reason, with a move-on-when-ready/mastery-based system, if they can acquire the necessary credits to graduate by age 16, the regulations allow them to do so.

The combination of the flexibility in the new state regulations and the knowledge that students can no longer simply bide time until they are 16 to get out of school has proven to be an amazing combination. In 2011, New Hampshire's dropout rate fell to 4.68%.

FOLLOW THE SYSTEM VERSUS FOLLOW THE CHILD

Follow the System

We all know how the old system works. We've been following this system for longer than anyone reading this book has been alive. Students show up to school around the beginning of September. They are assigned homerooms and classes. Their classes are made up of the offerings made available by the school. At the high school level, those class offerings, generally, number in the 50 to 75 range.

Generally speaking, on day one, students open the books to chapter one, page one. It is the teacher's job to get through the book (approved curriculum) by the end of the school year in June.

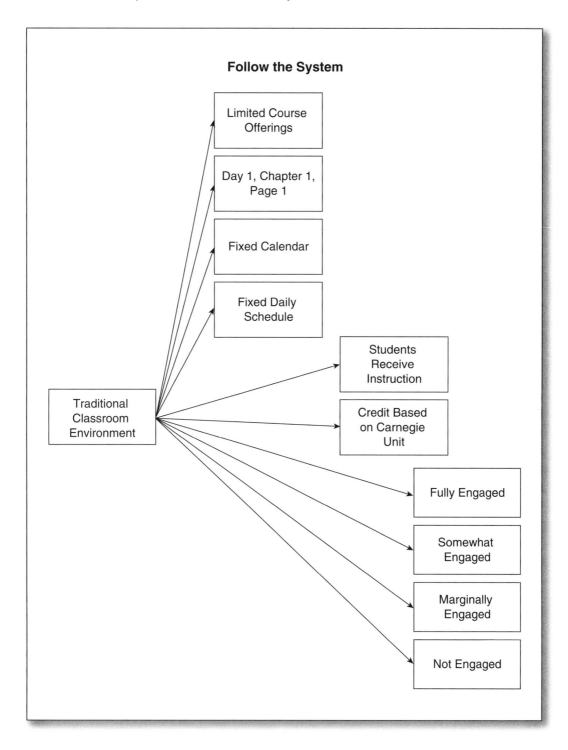

Follow the Child/Student

When Dr. Lyonel Tracy became commissioner of the New Hampshire Department of Education (2006), he introduced the concept of Follow the Child (QISA, 2009, p.1), which is a personalized whole-child approach to student learning. It includes unique (SASID) pupil identifiers in order to ensure the ability to collect, maintain, and use important data, even if students move from district to district.

Leading the Nation

A front-page article in the November 10, 2010, issue of *Foster's Daily Democrat* (Dover, New Hampshire, p.1), one of New Hampshire's daily newspapers, was titled, "New Hampshire's Leading Way in Lowering Dropout Rate, Boosting Graduation Rate" by Kyle Stucker (2010).

Here are some excerpts from the article:

- "A new study (Building a Grad Nation) shows New Hampshire is one of the states leading the way in reducing the country's overall high school dropout rate and increasing the overall graduation rate" (Stucker, 2010, p. 1).
- "District administrators have been able to reduce dropouts rates and increase overall graduation rates by becoming more flexible with students, dealing with individual students more directly to meet their needs, and increasing both the overall number and the types of options students have to complete high school" (Stucker, 2010, p. 1).
- "Jean Briggs Badger, the Dover superintendent, said her district has been able to decrease its dropout rate by increasing the number of alternative ways students can get their diplomas. 'I think it's that increased flexibility and doing whatever it takes to meet the needs of students on a case's by case basis,' said Badger" (Stucker, 2010, p. 1).
- "Rochester superintendent Mike Hopkins said his district has decreased its rate thanks to the 'lots of options for students'" (Stucker, 2010, p. 1).
- "Portsmouth assistant superintendent Steve Zadravec said, 'Districts need to keep pushing toward completely reducing the dropout rate. It's not enough to have a low dropout rate. I don't see us going back at this point'" (Stucker, 2010, p. 1).

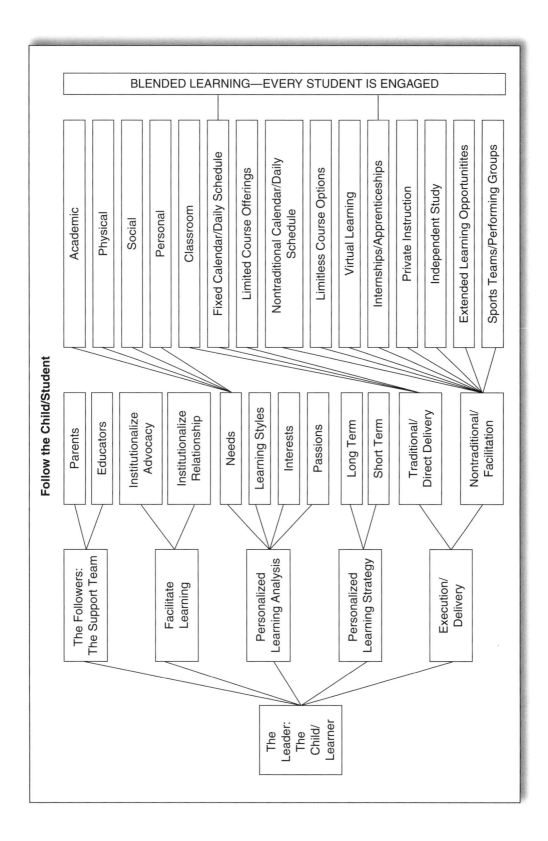

Follow the Child/Student

BLENDED LEARNING—EVERY STUDENT IS ENGAGED

Academic

Physical

Social

Personal

Classroom

Fixed Calendar/Daily Schedule

Limited Course Offerings

Nontraditional Calendar/Daily Schedule

Limitless Course Options

Virtual Learning

Internships/Apprenticeships

Private Instruction

Independent Study

Extended Learning Opportunitites

Sports Teams/Performing Groups

Parents

Educators

Institutionalize Advocacy

Institutionalize Relationship

Needs

Learning Styles

Interests

Passions

Long Term

Short Term

Traditional/ Direct Delivery

Nontraditional/ Facilitation

The Followers: The Support Team

Facilitate Learning

Personalized Learning Analysis

Personalized Learning Strategy

Execution/ Delivery

The Leader: The Child/ Learner

This is very powerful. These are the words of the local school leaders who are implementing more and more options for students—and it's working.

Points of engagement in learning for formerly disenfranchised learners often fall outside of the paradigms of traditional education. In shifting the paradigm to one of anytime, anyplace, anyhow, any pace learning, youth who, in the past, dropped out are now remaining engaged and are choosing to do so. In a competency-based learning model, in which mastery and personalization begin in early childhood education, student engagement is sustained over time on a pathway that leads to college-/ work-ready graduates.

10 Teacher Versus Educator

At the 2009 Austin Summit on Redefining Teacher Education for Digital Age Learners, education leaders from major education associations, universities, and departments of education around the country were gathered to help define the education skills necessary to bring public education into the 21st century. There were approximately 125 attendees, armed with Promethean personal responders and whiteboards, ready to answer the question on the skills of a 21st century educator. Attendees were given 22 choices to vote on, with 1 being the lowest value and 5 being the top value. It wasn't so much about what came in first of the 22 choices, but what came in last was startling.

The item that came in dead last, like a mule racing thoroughbreds, was "delivers content." Wait! Isn't that the primary role of teachers in America? Isn't that what teachers do? They "stand and deliver," as the 1988 movie depicting the story of East LA's Garfield High School's advanced calculus teacher, Jaime Escalante, suggests. If delivering content came in last place in importance in a 21st century education system, then we must redefine the role of a teacher. We are already more than 10% into the 21st century, yet delivering content is still the number-one role of our teachers.

To get an interesting perspective on why delivering content came in last, Google "Dan Brown education" (not the author) and watch the 8-minute video titled "An Open Letter to Educators" (Brown, 2010) of a 20-something-year-old college dropout talking about "institutional education" and why it is out of touch with a technological world. "Facts are free," Brown says, referencing that he only needs to go to the Internet to find information that is more comprehensive, faster, and more to his liking. He talks about textbooks that he never opens and teachers using

PowerPoints expecting students to regurgitate facts on a test to determine whether they learned those facts. He talks about how students don't need to be taught to memorize facts that the teacher spouts but how students need to become adept at 21st century skills (i.e., creativity, collaboration, communication, etc.).

The 2010 New Hampshire Summit on Redefining Educator Development for 21st Century Learners was among the important milestones in the process of moving our teachers into the process of thinking beyond teaching. While the 2005 changes in the state K–12 regulations may have begun this process, without subsequent supporting efforts, a change of this magnitude might take many decades to actualize. Just changing the regulations without subsequent support merely prolongs the change process.

Led by Dr. Robert McLaughlin, one of the Austin summit's planners, New Hampshire was the only state allowed to bring a team to the Austin summit. Dr. McLaughlin, a member of the New Hampshire Department of Education's higher education credentialing team, convinced the other summit planners that, because of New Hampshire's efforts around school redesign, the summit would be well served with a team from New Hampshire. The New Hampshire team referred to themselves as the Summiteers.

Upon return from Austin, the Summiteers, under Dr. McLaughlin's leadership, organized to form a planning team to create a similar summit in New Hampshire. In May 2010, the New Hampshire Summit on Redefining Educator Development for 21st Century Learners brought together teams from 14 of the 15 teacher-training institutions in New Hampshire. Each team needed to include K–12 members from school districts in their local areas. Many remarked that it was the first time anyone could recall K–12 and higher-ed people being brought together in such an effort.

PUTTING THE PIECES TOGETHER

The term *teacher*, in the traditional sense, implies that the individual is responsible for imparting knowledge and skills in the learning process. Generally, it is envisioned that this transfer of knowledge occurs inside of school classrooms. But if, as the Austin summit participants concluded, this process of teaching and learning is not likely to be how students learn in the 21st century, then what is the future role of those who we've referred to for centuries as *teachers*? New Hampshire has envisioned that this role will move from content delivery to facilitation of the process of learning. To lead this transformation, much work has gone into convincing stakeholders, discussing how this shift might best occur, changing regulations, holding conferences, and so forth. In using the term *educator*, we recognize that several individuals are sharing the role of causing learning to occur. A community mentor while a student is engaged in an extended learning opportunity, a certified educator in a particular content area, an online teacher in a virtual course, a guidance counselor working with a student in career and personal counseling—each has a role as an educator in a learner's pathway. This section is intended to show how New Hampshire is building upon this notion of moving from teachers to facilitators of learning.

Policymakers at the state level must review all aspects of current rules and procedures relating to school, college, and university approval, educator certification, and educator-preparation programs in support of the vision for anytime, anyplace, anyhow, any pace, competency-based learning. Simplifying this code of law is as much needed as simplifying the tax code in the United States. Creating a simpler code of educational law that supports this common vision is a key element in moving all schools forward in redesigning local learning opportunities. In order for shareholders to design new learning systems at the local level, shaping policy at the state level that is reflective of competency-based mastery is critical. The process must be driven by the regulatory agencies in a well-thought-out, coordinated effort that will ensure systemwide change at all levels.

REVAMPING THE MINIMUM STANDARDS FOR PUBLIC SCHOOL APPROVAL (THE 306s), 2005

When the New Hampshire State Board of Education changed the K–12 regulations, removing the Carnegie Unit, moving away from a time-based system to a competency-based system, and allowing anytime, anyplace, anyhow, any pace learning for credit toward graduation, it made a move unprecedented in America to enter the 21st century in education. But rulemaking alone does not a 21st century educator make. While this was a giant first step, it was still only a first step. The foundation for this book was created when New Hampshire made those changes to the Minimum Standards document in 2005.

NEW HAMPSHIRE VISION FOR HIGH SCHOOL REDESIGN DOCUMENT, 2007: MOVING FROM HIGH SCHOOLS TO LEARNING COMMUNITIES

The New Hampshire vision for high school redesign (New Hampshire Department of Education, 2007) document was crafted in order to provide a clearer understanding of the spirit and intent behind the changes in the

Minimum Standards (2005) and included a section called "Moving from Teachers to Learning Facilitators."

> Teachers should transition from a traditional delivery approach toward coaching, mentoring, and facilitating student learning. As learning facilitators, teachers become more active designers of curriculum. They encourage students to assume responsibility for their learning and move from teacher-centered to student-centered education. The transition to new roles for teachers will require a strong professional development effort, but will lead to more exciting and rewarding careers for teachers. (New Hampshire Department of Education, 2007, p. 2)

NEW HAMPSHIRE SUMMIT ON DEVELOPING 21ST CENTURY EDUCATORS, 2010

Following up on the Austin summit (2009), New Hampshire was the first state in the United States to hold a similar summit on developing 21st century educators. Once again, look at the comments from the summit to see the reinforcement of the message of moving away from teaching and toward facilitating learning.

The following are excerpts from the comments of various presenters and panelists at the 2010 New Hampshire Summit on Redefining Educator Development for 21st Century Learners.

Karen Soule, Chair, New Hampshire Professional Standards Board

- It's not about the teaching, it's really about the learning and we have to change some of our habits. Policies are what are going to drive this.

Tom Carroll, President, National Commission on Teaching and America's Future

- What matters most in the 21st century is less teaching and more learning.
- Schools of education need to get out of the teacher preparation business.
- You need to be in the educator talent development business. You need to get out of the teacher preparation business and you need to do it fast because the world around you is changing including the education world around you.

Fred recalls: Holy mackerel! Tom Carroll just told all of our teacher-preparation programs that they need to get out of the teacher-preparation business. At first, I was concerned about how they would react. But the reaction has been, for the most part, positive, and New Hampshire continues to bring Dr. Carroll back to assist in transforming educator development.

- We have to get out of this idea that we are going to staff schools with single stand-alone teachers in classrooms and start creating learning teams.
- What would these teachers need to do? They will develop learning-age competencies.
  - *Core competencies:* in language arts, reasoning, information, literacy, mathematics, science, and social sciences necessary for college and workforce success
  - *Creative competencies:* including creative expression in the arts, critical thinking, innovative and collaborative problem solving, and resourcefulness
  - *Communication competencies:* with languages, digital media, social networking, and content-creation technologies
  - *Cultural competencies:* including cultural understanding, personal and communal responsibility, adaptability and resilience, and ability to engage in production teamwork and active citizen participation
- These are not things that you teach. These are not things that you learn from a textbook. These are things that you learn by doing in collaborative teams in competency-based learning environments.
- So, the teachers need to learn to facilitate this competency development in their students, but the teachers also need to develop these competencies.
- If you're serious about getting out of teacher preparation in education talent development, what talents do they need to develop? These are talents they need to have.
- You need to ask yourself, are your graduates leaving with those competencies?
- In education, we immediately see *personalized* and we think it's the teacher's job to personalize the learning for the student and tailor the learning to the student. No, it's the learner's job to personalize the learning and it's the teacher's job to facilitate that personalization.
- Three Ways to Develop Educators (only one leads to the future):

1. Design campus-based teacher preparation improvements with new courses and programs … to prepare better stand-alone teachers who deliver text-based instruction in yesterday's self-contained classrooms.

(Continued)

(Continued)

2. Create new partnerships with mentored induction programs, professional development schools, teaching coaches, and innovative technologies...to develop better stand-alone teachers who deliver text-based instruction in yesterday's self-contained classrooms.

3. Replace teacher preparation with educator talent development from career pipelines to career lattices that support mass career customization. From preparing teachers to developing learning experts and learning facilitators. Educator development becomes project-based learning in which the project is to learn how to facilitate learning.

In the first two scenarios, you haven't changed anything.

- Prepare learning experts, learning facilitators, and make educator development be project-based learning.
- What if one of the students knows more than the certified teacher?
- It's no longer classroom based...it's project-based learning.
- So, we just have to simultaneously change the business model. If we try to piecemeal it, we'll get stuck.
- With the massive shift we have going on in our economy, this kind of change could happen in 5–8 years.

John Shea, Past Principal, Spaulding High School, Rochester, New Hampshire; Cofounder High Tech High, San Diego, California

- Schools of education can't prepare teachers to go off into high schools that don't exist and high schools can't do things differently until we start getting folks coming out of teacher education programs that are prepared to do things differently. We have to partner.

Dr. Phil Littlefield, Superintendent, Hooksett, New Hampshire

- We need to revisit the master teacher certification, redefine it from a competency-based point of view.

Dr. Chris Dede, Wirth Professor on Learning Technologies, Harvard University

- So, imagine the educational system, where outside of school hours, outside of the custodial function, there are parent tutors, informal education coaches, and community mentors that are part of the formal education. They're paid, they're licensed, and they work in complement with teachers.

- And schools of education are different because now you're not just preparing teachers, you're preparing tutors and coaches and mentors all together in a rich kind of orchestration.

Dr. Milton Chen, Senior Fellow, George
Lucas Education Foundation

- What they are doing outside of the school context can be brought into schools of education, into your courses and into your teacher development.
- I do believe that these digital learners are carrying this change in their pockets, just as you are. By carrying these digital devices, with access to the Internet, we totally transform where, when, and how learning happens.
- When learners are leading their own learning—that's what we want.

Dr. Paul Resta, Professor of Instructional
Technology, University of Texas, Austin, Texas

- We need to realize that technology is changing, knowledge is changing, the learners are changing, but is teacher education changing?
- Many policymakers are not seeing teacher education institutions as part of the solution but, perhaps, part of the problem. We need to change that. If teacher education doesn't do this, it's very clear that others will.

Stephen Jury, Promethean World PLC

- The nonroutine interactive and nonroutine analytical skills are the skill sets that will be increasingly in demand in the future.
- The ones that are easy to teach in terms of cognitive skills are the ones that are easy to outsource.

CREATION OF AN IHE (INSTITUTIONS OF HIGHER EDUCATION) NETWORK, 2011

During the opening remarks of the May 2010 New Hampshire Summit on Developing 21st Century Educators, Dr. Robert McLaughlin (McLaughlin, 2010) told the attendees of the four goals of the summit. One of the goals was the creation of an IHE network in order for our 15 state teacher-preparation programs to begin working with each other to create models for training teachers in order to move beyond teaching and into a 21st century learning mode, in which, hopefully, they would engage in sharing their development.

This was an important step in bringing all of New Hampshire's teacher-training institutions together for the purpose of rethinking how we train educators to work in and help create 21st century schools. Since the first summit in May 2010, the IHEs have continued to meet and collaborate.

With growing financial pressures on districts, local school boards will seek candidates who have the credentialed depth of knowledge and actual field experience to move to a more cost-effective model that holds the promise of raising the bar for students. IHEs will need to begin the process of creating undergraduate and graduate degrees in competency-based learning. This will become the hot degree program for educators in the next decade or so as districts try to find individuals who are skilled at transitioning from a time-based model.

REVAMPING OF TEACHER/EDUCATOR PREPARATIONS PROGRAMS REGULATIONS (THE 600s REGULATIONS), 2011

New teacher training regulations have been passed by the State Board of Education (2011). The 600s have been totally revamped to reflect moving away from full-time content delivery in classrooms and toward facilitator, coach, and mentor in move-on-when-ready/anytime, anyplace, anyhow, any pace learning environments. These new regulations will change how New Hampshire IHEs shape their preparation programs.

The following rule-making language (see box) was developed using the basic structure of the latest InTASC standards (Council of Chief State School Officers, 2011), then "New Hampshirized" to fit with the anytime, anyplace, anyhow, any pace direction of the New Hampshire Department of Education and State Board of Education. The irony of using these standards as a basis for how New Hampshire views the future preparation of its teachers is that the word *teacher*, along with *classroom* and *instruction*, has been largely eliminated from the document.

ED 610.02 *Professional Education Requirements.* To promote the learning of all students, each professional educator preparation program shall require each graduate of the program to demonstrate evidence of the following:

A. In the area of the learner and learning:

1. Learner development, as demonstrated by:

   a. An understanding of how learners develop, recognizing that patterns of learning and development vary individually within and across the personal, physical, social, and academic dimensions; and
   b. The ability to facilitate developmentally appropriate and challenging learning experiences based on the unique needs of each learner.

2. Learning differences, as demonstrated by:

   a. An understanding of individual differences and diverse cultures and communities;
   b. Ensuring inclusive environments that allow each learner to reach his or her full potential; and
   c. The ability to employ universal design principles and assistive technology.

3. Learning environment, as demonstrated by:

   a. Working with learners to create and access learning environments that support self-directed individual and collaborative learning, based on each learner's interests and passions; and
   b. Use of learning environments not limited to the classroom, but extended into the larger community as well as virtual experience.

B. In the area of content:

1. Content knowledge, as demonstrated by:

   a. An understanding of the central concepts, tools of inquiry, and structure of his or her discipline(s); and
   b. An ability to create learning experiences that make the disciplines(s) accessible and meaningful for learners.

2. Innovative applications of content, as demonstrated by:

   a. An understanding of how to connect concepts and use differing perspectives to engage learners in critical and creative thinking and collaborative problem solving related to authentic local and global issues.

(Continued)

(Continued)

C. In the area of learning facilitation practice:

1. Use of assessment as demonstrated by:

a. An understanding and ability to use multiple methods of assessment to:

- Engage learners in their own growth;
- Document learner progress;
- Provide learner feedback; and
- Inform the educator's ongoing planning and instructional practices.

2. Planning for learning facilitation, as demonstrated by:

a. An ability, as an active member of a learning community, to draw upon knowledge of content area standards, cross-disciplinary skills, learners, the community, and pedagogy to plan learning experiences that support every learner in meeting rigorous learning goals.

3. Learning facilitation strategies, as demonstrated by:

a. An understanding and use of a variety of strategies and tools to encourage learners to develop deep understanding of content areas and their connections to other disciplines; and

b. An ability to build skills in accessing, applying, and communicating information.

D. In the area of professional responsibility:

1. Reflection and continuous growth, as demonstrated by:

a. Being a reflective practitioner and using evidence to continually evaluate his or her practice, particularly the effects of choices and actions on students, families, and other professionals in the learning community; and

b. Ability to adapt practice to meet the needs of each learner.

2. Collaboration, as demonstrated by:

a. Collaborating, as a member of the larger learning community, with learners, families, colleagues, other professionals, and community members to leverage resources that contribute to student growth and development, learning, and well-being.

Source: Council of Chief State School Officers, 2011.

REVAMPING EDUCATOR DEVELOPMENT PROGRAM REGULATIONS (THE 500s), 2011

These regulations were passed by the State Board of Education (December 2011). These new regulations will change how we develop our professional educators. Please note the similarities between this draft language and the competencies as presented by Dr. Thomas Carroll at the 2010 New Hampshire Summit on Redefining Educator Development for 21st Century Learners (New Hampshire Department of Education, 2010).

Ed 505.06 *General Education Certification Requirements.* Each applicant who seeks certification under Ed 505.04 shall have completed a program providing the following core competencies.

A. Content competencies in the following areas necessary for college and workforce access:

1. Language arts;

2. Reasoning;

3. Information literacy;

4. Mathematics;

5. Sciences; and

6. Social studies.

B. Creative competencies in the following areas:

1. Creative expression;

2. Critical thinking;

3. Innovative and collaborative problem solving; and

4. Resourcefulness.

C. Communication competencies in the following areas:

1. Languages;

2. Digital media;

3. Networking; and

4. "Content-creation" technologies.

(Continued)

(Continued)

    D. Cultural competencies in the following areas:

        1. Cultural understanding;

        2. Taking responsibility for self and others;

        3. Adaptability and resilience;

        4. Ability to engage in productive teamwork; and

        5. Social and civic engagement.

Source: Council of Chief State School Officers, 2011.

While no New Hampshire IHE has a fully developed 21st century educator program, some programs are fairly advanced and are aggressively moving forward.

What will a 21st century educator development program look like?

MODIFICATION OF THE MINIMUM STANDARDS FOR PUBLIC SCHOOL APPROVAL, 2011

As stated previously, the Minimum Standards for Public School Approval is the guiding regulatory document for K–12 education in New Hampshire. While the entire Minimum Standards document was not opened up for a full revamping by the New Hampshire State Board of Education, a select number of items were brought forward by the New Hampshire Department of Education for clarification and assistance in making true school transformation a reality at the district level. Under the bold leadership of Commissioner Virginia Barry and Deputy Commissioner Paul Leather, assisted by the tremendous work of a group of school administrators, the new changes to the Minimum Standards (December 2011) have landmark potential.

Fred recalls: In 2004, the Standards Task Force was wrestling with various issues in the proposed changes to the Minimum Standards. While I was quite pleased with the progress of the group, I lost one of my arguments. The argument was over the regulation regarding the number of course offerings required for every high school. The regulations stated that every high school needed to make available a minimum of 45 course offerings (most high schools offered significantly more that 45 offerings) and, further, defined them by subject areas. I suggested to the group that we eliminate this regulation because with the changes that we had already agreed upon, including allowing online courses, internships, apprenticeships, work study, sports teams, performing groups, independent study, and the like to be available as credit-bearing opportunities, the number 45 was virtually meaningless. The union representatives balked at the suggestion.

So instead, I tried to take the opposite approach. I said, "Okay, if you don't want to eliminate it, I propose that we make the number 450." There was a look of bewilderment on their faces. I lost the argument. The number remained at 45.

In 2010, Ed Murdough, the Department of Education person charged with overseeing compliance on the Minimum Standards, was approached by administrators who were asking for clarification on this issue. They asked Ed to show where in the document that it said that they couldn't just offer 45 online courses to meet the standard. He replied that he did not believe that such action would meet the spirit of what the board was trying to accomplish. So, with the input of school administrators, the following proposal to change the language around required course offerings passed into regulation in December 2011.

ED 306.27-High School Curriculum, Credits, Graduation Requirements, and Cocurricular Program

A. The 13.5 program specific credits (core courses) required for high school graduation in Ed 306.24(m) not including open electives and information communicating technology, shall be offered in a classroom setting. Duplicate equivalent or additional courses in these programs areas may be offered through distance education, extended learning opportunities, or other alternative methods.

Simply stated, the only high school courses that the state now requires to be in classrooms are those core 13.5 math, language arts, science, and social studies courses required for graduation. However, if students don't want to take these and want to master the competencies in another way, they can. This means that the state no longer requires that the arts, physical education, and so on be offered in traditional classroom settings. While schools will still be required to offer 45 program-specific, credit-bearing choices, it becomes a local decision on how to offer them. The significance of this change cannot be overstated.

11 Teacher Compensation

There's an iconic scene in the movie *Indiana Jones and the Raiders of the Lost Ark* in which the hero, Indy, is chased through the bazaar with the villains hot on his heels. All of a sudden, he is confronted with the baddest of the bad guys, a larger-than-life swordsman swathed in black, brandishing his saber, artfully displaying his deadly skills. The exhausted Indy appears doomed. Will his bullwhip be a match for this deadly foe? Can he flee? In a moment, the concerned look on Indy's face transforms into a sly, "why didn't I think of this before?" grin. Jones reaches into his pocket, pulls out a gun, shoots the swordsman, shrugs, and turns away—triumphant.

Beyond the pure entertainment of this famous scene, there's an important lesson to be learned: use the right tools at the right time. In this example, the once-vaunted saber of centuries past was vanquished by modernity in the form of a pistol, and what may have been the efficient, effective tool once upon a time was dispatched by a newer solution that rendered the earlier one obsolete. Our education system is no different, and we are at a "Why didn't we think of this before?" moment. Moving from a time-based system to a competency-based, anytime, anywhere system is the effective delivery system of learning for the 21st century.

While New Hampshire has been very successful in making dramatic changes to its state regulations, the actual transformation is not nearly as dramatic as it could be because too many time-based supports are still in place. These time-based supports, in large part, include school calendars, report cards, daily schedules, tenure, seniority, and even the basic tenets of how we compensate our teachers.

A teacher's contract is one of the most entrenched support structures of a time-based system. In America, we pay our teachers for time. If they are considered full-time teachers, their contracts are based on performing their tasks during specific hours of the day, week, and year, generally 7:30 a.m. to 3:00 p.m. for 180 days a year. If teachers are asked to work longer hours or more days, their contracts generally specify that they must be paid for their time. Is this a fair thing to do? Certainly it is if teachers are time-based employees. A more intriguing question is whether teachers should be time-based employees.

In New Hampshire, under the new regulations, some districts have changed their calendars and their daily schedules, some have changed their report cards to competency-based report cards, and with the passage of New Hampshire Senate Bill 196 (Relative to the Renomination or Reelection of Teachers and Grievance Procedures, 2011), the state government has changed New Hampshire's so-called tenure law (RSA-189:14-a, 2011). But, for the most part, the general structure of a teacher's contract looks pretty much the same as it has for decades.

A 21ST CENTURY SOLUTION

A true competency-based, anytime, anyplace, anyhow, any pace school environment will be market driven in the sense that the students and their parents will be primary drivers in making decisions on how students learn. Traditionally, when school systems have limited offerings, the only choice for students is the traditional classroom experience. The administration ensures that virtually every teacher's class has a reasonable number of students, therefore avoiding the appearance that taxpayer dollars are being used inefficiently.

But in a true anytime, anyplace, system, the world becomes open and accessible for students to turn it into valid learning experiences. In this learning environment, if a teacher's class is filled with students, it's because, regardless of the great number of options in community settings or online, the students choose to be in this teacher's class. At the same time, another teacher may not have fared as well. Despite it being a part of a public school system, this concept of offering more choices than ever before, especially in the early stages of change, will be unsettling to many teachers.

Rose: In a recent conversation with a music teacher in a high school that has moved to competency-based learning and grading, the teacher reflected on how difficult the recent school year of transformation was for him. He is one of those "superstar" music teachers who can respond to student interests and needs and creates a wonderful chorus experience for both young men and women. He reflected that once he had to teach his chorus class with course competencies, it became a source of conflict with some of his students. Clearly, he noted that, in the past, chorus attracted some students who may not enjoy the typical school academics but enjoy musical expression in its many forms. However, once competencies were invoked, it took the fun out of the course for some of these students. Some students simply participated, yet chose not to pursue the assessments of the competencies, settling for poor grades.

This teacher was concerned that these disinterested students would no longer sign up for chorus. Lack of student demand in a course could lead to teacher layoffs, and this teacher was concerned for his job. In coaching him, I tried to stretch his thinking a bit. Does participation in a course in school always have to yield a credit? Could students have such choice? I hope so. This teacher is a dynamic, student-centered teacher who sees his role as an educator evolving in this new learning environment. We have to ensure that this system we are changing also provides the encouragement and support for our effective educators to change their traditional roles while minimizing their fears.

So, what should be the role of the school if there is a great student demand for the services of one teacher and a clear lack of demand for the services of another? Is it the school's role to balance student loads, as it has in the past? This clearly benefits teachers whose services may receive low or no demand from students. Is that the right thing to do for students, or is that the system, once again, imposing its will upon the students? If we want students to take ownership of their learning, we have to let them make choices and must do our best to respect those choices. But, if many of the choices that the students have are disappointing choices . . . sounds like 20th century again.

Twenty-first century choices are virtually limitless. The only way they become limited is if the system puts limits on them. This will inevitably occur early on in the transformation process as the system pushes back to try to fend off transformation.

Fred recalls: The daughter of a close friend of mine was struggling at her high school. I've known this young lady since birth. She told me how much she disliked school. She also said that she would like to learn to speak Swedish. I spoke to the high school principal, who gave me a number of excuses for why they could not make this happen. The excuses included statements like, "We don't have anyone who can properly assess her progress," "How can we be sure that an online course is a good course?" to "We don't want to upset our faculty by approving these outside-of-school experiences." A few years later, in a letter from that same high school principal, the principal spoke with pride of opening the door to extended learning opportunities.

Some limits may, of course, be valid. For example, online courses or community offerings devoted to witchcraft, bomb making, or Nazism are not likely to become approved school offerings without a very convincing argument by students and parents. In other cases, adjustments may be needed to ensure that an offering meets required competencies. Let's say, for example, that a real-world science (chemistry) offering is made available in a science-based business but, of the six competencies that the school requires, only four will be mastered in this environment, and this extended learning opportunity does not address the other two competencies. Should the school reject this offering? Absolutely not! The educator overseeing this student's work must find other ways to address the remaining competencies and take responsibility to ensure that this student will achieve mastery before credit is granted.

As we fine-tune this approach, we expect the number of purely classroom-based courses to decrease as time passes; only the best ones will survive. As with the above chemistry example, many classroom offerings will become blended into combinations of classroom, online, and real world. The inherent flexibility of this system will enable the creativity of great teachers to be unleashed in order to create exciting blended learning experiences, and students will flock to them. Some traditional offerings may disappear sooner than others. World languages that currently are available in our course offering as a 4- or 5-year experience may be reduced to far less classroom time given the availability of high-quality virtual learning and experiential opportunities to gain competency. This will result in students experiencing more languages than the few languages offered in the traditional courses at the high school level, which are constrained by cost of hiring staff for full-year contracts and classroom space considerations.

WHY THE OLD COMPENSATION SCHEME WON'T WORK

Never underestimate the power of the inertia of the 20th century, time-based model. In this clash of centuries, the old pay-for-time system will not go away easily. New Hampshire is already more than one half decade past the changes in the state's regulations, which mandate moving from a time-based system to a competency-based system, yet the actual, tangible evidence of change for too many districts is often difficult to find.

One key change that has yet to happen anywhere in New Hampshire is a change from a time-based compensation system to a competency-based model. It's almost as if there is a sense that, if we ignore this component of a competency-based system long enough, maybe no one will say anything. At some point, this issue must be dealt with, because the nature of a time-based compensation system will undercut the essence of a competency-based system of educating our students. A time-based system is designed to judge students' performance at fixed periods of time and to then move on to the next lessons whether or not the student has actually learned. That contradicts the entire purpose of a competency-based model. If teachers are contractually finished working at the end of the year yet have not sufficiently brought a number of their students to mastery, the hope for a true competency-based education model will be doomed as yet another failure in the long line of attempts at reforming public education.

If we, the members of the public education system in America, do not put a 100% effort into working to perfect this new model, we will put public education at more risk than it is already. There are plenty of forces out there that revile public education, that believe public education to be another failed attempt at socialism, that have real stories, personal and family stories, that fuel their distaste for public education, and they are not all wrong. There exist among the ranks of our locally and nationally elected lawmakers and local taxpayer organizations individuals who see public education as the enemy. Their views should not be summarily dismissed as "a bunch of right-wing crackpots." The basic structure of how public education compensates its employees opens itself up for criticism like "Where else in America does everyone get paid the same amount regardless of their performance?" While we cannot fix the past, we can fix the future. We hold on to these underpinnings of an obsolete system at our (public education's) own risk.

We must transition to a new compensation system, but what will it look like?

COMPENSATION: FROM CARNEGIE TO COMPETENCY

If teachers can get their students to achieve mastery of competencies in less than the traditional time frame, how should they be compensated? With near-limitless opportunities to bring students to mastery, especially with technology, many of those traditional kill-and-drill, stand-and-deliver approaches will be replaced by online offerings, enabling our educators to spend their time with students who have already gotten the facts online and are now learning to use their newfound knowledge in real-world ways facilitated by 21st century educators. This has profound implications for teacher compensation.

As we all know, the standard compensation schedule of the 20th century is based on an individual's number of years teaching and level of college degree attainment (i.e., master's, PhD). The unions approve of it because, in their view, it seems fair. There's nothing arbitrary or capricious about it . . . or is there? While this is a fairly simple system to calculate, will it make sense in a competency-based world?

Fred recalls: I met my wife, Bette, during my teaching stint at Dolan Middle School. She was an English teacher. I remember wanting to go out on a date one night, and she told me that she couldn't because she had too many papers to correct. Well, that wasn't a good enough answer for me. So I suggested that I go over to her apartment to see if there was any way that I could help her. I arrived to find a mountain of handwritten essays from students that needed to be assessed for content, style, structure, spelling, grammar, and so on—all of the things that an English teacher needs to do to help students learn to write. I was floored! I knew of the afterschool workload that I had as a science teacher and began thinking about the afterschool workloads of other teachers. The physical education teachers actually got paid to coach teams after school. But the English/language arts teachers . . . OMG! While the daytime hours may have been uniform, the overall workload was definitely not equal and was interfering with my ability to make time with my girlfriend.

Time-based issues like tenure and seniority and even added compensation for advanced degrees attained will likely become minimized in a competency-based system. If students choose options that have nothing to do with how long someone has been in the system or their degrees, what expectations will individuals or the unions have for the system to keep them financially whole, protecting their status and their salary? The future value of advanced degrees for educators will be in preparing individuals to become more highly skilled at helping students learn and, as a direct result, be able to create quality offerings that will be highly attractive to school districts and students. The likelihood is that if there is little or no demand for an individual's services, there will likely be a self-realization that things will probably not work out well, and people will need to either find ways to make their offerings more attractive or simply move on.

Will educators be paid on a uniform salary schedule in a competency-based system? Possibly, but if so, the salary schedule will likely be based on other factors such as an individual's impact on student performance—more specifically, a demonstrated ability to bring students to mastery of competencies, not a salary schedule based on years of service and number of degrees.

How will this work? School districts will contract with individuals who will be charged with the task of bringing students to mastery of competencies and achieving the other goals of the district. Those goals might include student advocacy, like getting students into great colleges; whole-child needs, not just academic needs, but social, physical, personal needs; and whole-community needs, including the successful harnessing of community resources. While all of this may be considered in hiring decisions and become a part of an educator's job description, from the district's viewpoint, they will consider all of this a part of the job of bringing students to mastery of competencies. While currently districts look at cost per student, in the future, districts will likely look at "cost per credit attainment" (Gary Hunter, personal conversation, 2011). Our teaching institution will transition from developing "stand-alone teachers for stand-alone classrooms" (Carroll, 2010) to creating learning experts, individuals whose skills are anchored by facility in getting students to learn in anytime, anyplace, anyhow, at any pace learning environments.

BAD TEACHERS?

In the not-so-distant past, unacceptable teacher performance was not easy to identify or quantify because of inadequate teacher supervision and evaluation. Teachers, in large part, looked like they were doing their jobs well. Obviously, there were students who were not doing well, but was that the teachers' fault or the students' fault? If another teacher had the same students, would the results be any different?

Today, it's not as easy for unacceptable results to remain unnoticed. Many spotlights shine on public education. Study after study shows that the differences between good and bad teacher performance can be enormous. Thus, there is a hue and cry to remove ineffective teachers.

While there are ongoing efforts to either remove bad teachers or find candidates from the top third of the college pool, we are probably looking at the wrong metrics to solve this problem. We have candidates who have chosen education as their profession for a reason, and we need to make sure they can be successful. In large part, educators are wonderful people who care deeply about doing a good job and came to the profession with an idealism to inspire and motivate young people. Oftentimes, the system itself sucks that enthusiasm out of them, and we end up with a number of good, caring people who are simply not skilled enough to be great at the task we've asked them to perform. If you haven't been a teacher, you might not know what it's like to keep 20 to 30 students with different learning styles, interests, skill sets, and so forth seated in one place when many would rather be somewhere else doing something else. This profession often requires skills similar to those needed for herding cats. And if you are not skilled at getting students to want to be in that classroom space, it is likely that you will be only marginally proficient at the job of teaching.

For a moment, please consider that it may not be that the teacher pool is made up of too many less-than-skilled professionals but, instead, that we are asking these good people to do the unnatural task of inspiring students who would rather be doing something else. What if, instead of trying to get rid of so-called bad teachers or seeking to find large pools of better teachers, we change the task to a more effective task, one that meets students where they want to be, doing what they want to do, inspiring them to attain a high level of competency through doing more of what they are inclined to do anyway? Isn't the more logical approach to take the army that we have and train them to be the army that we need for the future: performing a task that will likely be easier for these good people to become highly successful?

But are there bad teachers in public education? Of course there are, just like there are bad doctors, lawyers, and so on. The education documentary movie *Waiting for Superman* (Guggenheim, 2011) claims that 1 of every 57 doctors loses his/her license to practice, 1 out of every 97 lawyers loses his/her license, yet, only 1 of every 2,500 teachers loses his/her license to teach. On the surface, that sounds like a pretty damning statement about the profession's ability to police itself. But until we use different measurement tools, we will continue to get the same results. For this reason, there is increasing public pressure to make student performance a significant part of the criteria for how teachers are judged.

In 2011, the New Hampshire School Boards Association and School Administrators Association were successful in convincing the legislature to change the so-called tenure law to 5 years instead of 3 and also took away one avenue of appeal. Will this solve the problem with bad teachers? Probably not. The change in the tenure laws or changes in state regulations regarding dismissal of bad teachers, while better than nothing, are 20th century solutions to what is now a 21st century problem.

For many, the results of high-stakes tests are still seen as the ultimate measure of student performance. As a direct result, we are seeing allegations of huge cheating scandals (i.e., Atlanta public schools involving 200 teachers and principals) because of this intense pressure for students to perform on a test. In many ways, this pressure to improve student performance is breaking the back of the old system, and, for better or for worse, is likely here to stay. While teachers can offer critical input on how best to measure student performance, an analysis of teacher performance should include a variety of measures that include pedagogy, student growth, expertise, and input from peers, administrators, parents, and students. Although student performance will be a major factor in how educators are judged, a multifaceted approach to educator performance analysis will paint a clearer picture.

Fred recalls: At the CESA #1 (Cooperative Education Service Agency #1), Wisconsin, conference called Our Defining Moment, the Deconstruction and Transformation of Public Education, one of my presentations was to approximately 100 high school students. I asked the students, "How many of you have some absolutely wonderful teachers whose classes are exciting and who, you know, care about you and your education?" Virtually every student raised his or her hand. I then asked, "How many of you have some absolutely boring teachers and ones who you don't believe care about you and your education?" Again, virtually every student raised his or her hand.

Think about your own educational experiences. You, no doubt, had your own opinions about good and bad teachers. When you look back today through your adult eyes, would you guess that you were mostly right or wrong? Regardless, as currently structured, opportunities for the average student to avoid so-called bad teachers are not readily apparent.

But are these teachers truly bad teachers, or are many of them just burned out by a system that crushed their enthusiasm for the profession? We believe that, for many, it is possible that the idealism that brought them to this profession in the first place can be rekindled by a more logical approach to educate students. In any case, student performance will play a larger role in how we judge educators in the near and foreseeable future and will, ultimately, have a significant influence on how we compensate our professional educators.

The era of No Child Left Behind has created a greater demand for effectiveness in providing high-quality supervision and evaluation of teachers. This is very evident in the funding mechanisms for Race to the Top. At issue in many schools is the fact that some school leaders may not be the best instructional leaders to properly supervise and evaluate teachers. Oftentimes, the selection process for principals and assistant principals focuses more on school-management potential than on instruction and learning expertise.

For the most part, on any staff, the students, the community, and the school leaders know the great teachers. The students, the community, and the school leaders also know the ineffective teachers. Failure to show growth to greatness generally has not been part of supervision or evaluation systems in schools. The skill set of school leaders to move mediocre teachers to become great educators will be a factor in the ability to improve schools.

Consider the damage done to our learners by having an ineffective teacher for a full school year. Imagine if a principal, once realizing the ineffectiveness of a newly hired teacher, could simply release the individual mid-year and hire a better teacher. Our current system of teacher contracts gives probationary teachers full-year contracts. In most employment situations in the private sector, probationary periods are measured in days, not months or years. The notion of knowing that a teacher is ineffective yet allowing that individual to remain in place for a full school year should be unacceptable to all. In a competency-based system, a full year of ineffective teaching could set students back on the road to mastery. We know it is happening now. Does anyone find this acceptable? None of us should.

However, our goal should be to move away from this punitive "get rid of bad teachers" environment to one that encourages and trains our professionals to transform from deliverers of content in classrooms to facilitators of learning in the real world of the 21st century.

FULL TIME, PART TIME, OR FULL TIME PLUS

While some teachers may only want to perform their duties for 180 days, some teachers will want to do more, and others will want to do less. Should we let teachers choose to do more or less? If a teacher wants to do more and, ultimately, make more money, should he/she be allowed to do so, or should pay be restricted by a fixed schedule? The fixed schedule/ fixed compensation system of the 20th century works, in large part, because virtually the entire full-time faculty is contractually obliged to work the same schedule. While the uniform work schedule is a fixture in districts across America, it will begin to disappear as our skilled professionals move to an anytime, anyplace system.

Currently, there are 20th century, union-approved teacher contracts that allow teachers to earn more money for doing more. This thinking will become more and more prevalent in the 21st century. Will unions be able to find competency-based ways to formulate a new type of uniform pay scale?

Ultimately, in a 21st century compensation model, making more money would have much to do with the demand for that teacher's services. And if there was a demand for a teacher's services yet the teacher wanted to limit his/her availability, as so many Baby Boomer teachers nearing retirement might want, should that option be available to them in order that their work schedule is based on their terms, including their timetable? If school is still 180 days, 7:30 a.m. to 3:00 p.m., an administrator might say, "Thanks, but no thanks. It just won't work." But if the norm becomes learning anytime, anyplace, a new compensation model must emerge.

The reality, especially at the secondary level, may be a reduced demand for a particular teacher's services. Let's assume that this teacher still wants to teach full time. What does that person do now? Simply demanding a full-time job when one may no longer be available is not going to accomplish the desired result. The new paradigm can work to one's detriment, but the flexibility and opportunity of this new system can work to one's benefit as well. Just as students will have near-limitless opportunities to learn, teachers will have more opportunities to teach, even though many of those teaching opportunities may look quite different than a traditional schedule.

The traditional time-based schedule will evolve into one with many new possibilities. These may include educators offering classes during nights, weekends, and summers; teaching online courses; facilitating extended learning opportunities; teaching college-level courses in high school; and teaching in more than one district. Once again, just as the 21st century will offer students the opportunity to learn anytime/anyplace, the possibility of teaching anytime/anyplace will also hold true. Given the opportunity, many teachers and students and their parents might prefer a different calendar than September through June. Similarly, given the opportunity, some teachers may prefer a different daily schedule than 7:30 a.m. to 3:00 p.m. As transformation takes root and many conventional times and places are replaced by unconventional schedules, the possibility that the number of hours that teachers are expected to teach may remain about the same, but where, when, and how they perform their tasks will change. Imagine if some teachers were so much in demand that they could dictate where, when, and how districts and students will be able to access their services. With the availability of learning for credit anytime/anyplace, some teachers may only want to teach nights and want winter off instead of the summer. All of these possibilities can fit comfortably in an anytime, anywhere system.

While this may sound unsettling for some, this shift may occur naturally as large numbers of Baby Boomer teachers retire and 21st century educators begin to emerge from our educator-development programs. Besides, becoming a 21st century educator is likely to be more fun and more personally rewarding.

So what will be the future definition of a full-time education position in a true competency-based environment? It's likely to be a year-round position, as it is in the rest of American society

THE EMERGENCE OF EDUPRENEURS

In America, the concept of job security and jobs for life is feeling more and more a thing of the past. The 2010 Bureau of Labor Statistics Survey estimated that the average person born from 1957 to 1964 has held 11 jobs between ages 18 and 44 (United States Department of Labor, BLS, 2010). Although school administrator positions often seem like revolving doors, in many senses, these rapid job changes have not largely been felt among teachers. In a competency-based system of public education, this may change as teachers see opportunities to become edupreneurs.

Entrepreneurs already exist in public education. Some have private businesses based on special needs, juvenile justice, technology, consulting services, and more. In some cases, multimillion-dollar businesses have been created. Additionally, in an anytime, anyplace system, with the elimination of the assumption of a 180-day schedule and the ability to move students along at different paces, different types of individuals, who, in the past, might not have been attracted to public education because of the traditional wage structure, will begin to see interesting, entrepreneurial possibilities. This entrepreneurialism will also present opportunities for entrepreneurial-minded educators and outside service agencies to create new ways to provide efficiency and quality to multiple school districts in ways that are more engaging for students than many traditionally offered inside classrooms. Districts will view these opportunities based on their quality and ability to ensure that students are brought to mastery of competencies with a careful eye on cost per credit attainment.

The potential exists for many educators to make comfortable livings in this new paradigm. While the concept of becoming well to do based on educating students in a public school environment may be offensive to some, we will need to get comfortable with this, because, in the end, it will likely be beneficial to the recipients of the learning, the students, and those who finance it, the taxpayers.

This will likely be a very different job than that of a traditional teacher. Districts will begin to look at ways to compensate learning experts in this new milieu in which learning, not teaching, is the coin of the realm.

Part IV

Selling the Concept

A Conscious Effort to Create Public Demand

> *"If I'd asked my customers what they wanted,*
> *they'd have said a faster horse."*
>
> —Henry Ford

Virtually every American knows that our system of public education needs to change, but change into what? Henry Ford's quote suggests that what the citizens would have asked for to help with their transportation needs was a better version of what they already had. In education, there is the same concern. For the most part, our citizens', especially our parents', only vision of a public education is one that looks very much like what our current teaching model looks like. They accept the visual of classrooms, regardless of whether it is working for their child because that is all that they see. They simply want the best possible version of that model, which generally translates into the best teachers, the best school environment, the best administrators. They rarely get their ideal. A faster horse for everyone is not often possible.

What is possible is the model depicted in this book. But how can we make this transition to a new model? At the May 2010 New Hampshire Summit on Developing 21st Century Educators held at Southern New Hampshire University, Nellie Mae Education Foundation president Nick Donohue told the audience that leaders need to "make a conscious effort to create public demand" (Donohue, 2010) for this new model.

The good news is that this concept is a fairly easy sell for a highly skilled, charismatic communicator who understands the concept from top to bottom and who is capable of building legions of supporters to help move the concept forward. The bad news is, there are serious concerns regarding how many of these leaders are actually out there.

What's likely is that there are growing numbers of talented leaders who are ready to embrace a new model that they can believe in and then would be willing to play a serious role in creating that public demand if they are well prepared. Unfortunately, the formalized training necessary to accomplish this enormous task barely exists anywhere in America.

It is a hope of the authors that this book becomes a starting point for beginning to formalize how to move from a time-based to a competency-based system and that the book's audience brings these leaders to the surface.

Fortunately, these charismatic leaders don't necessarily have to be educators. While it would be preferable if they were, what they need to be is credible leaders. They could be elected officials, they could be parents, they could be business leaders, they could be community leaders—and it's not impossible that they could be students.

12 Selling to Students and Parents

T his may be the easiest sell of all. Russ Quaglia's My Voice survey (Quaglia, 2009) shows that 48% of students say that school is boring. It's easy for anyone to understand that students would prefer learning experiences that are not boring. Students will accept this grand bargain: the raising of the achievement bar, through which credit will only be acquired upon a demonstration of mastery, in exchange for a student-driven, student-owned, anytime, anyplace, anyhow, any pace learning system.

> *Fred recalls: I asked approximately 100 high school students in Wisconsin (using Promethean personal responders) if they would favor moving to this new system allowing them to own their education, even if the bar of accomplishment would be raised. On a scale of 1 to 5 with 5 being the highest, 63% gave it a 5, 23% gave it a 4, and a total of only 5% gave it a 1 or 2.*

Some fear that parents, who have traditionally been ardent defenders of the public system and have regularly championed for more resources, will be difficult to convince to change to a different school model. Once again, the skills of the leader(s) charged with communicating what a new model will look like, including the logic of moving to a new system, are paramount.

Nellie Mae Education Foundation president Nick Donohue said at the May 2010 New Hampshire Summit on Developing 21st Century Educators, "We are the ones who are in love with our model. The customers are in love with their children. And all they want is our undivided attention on building promising futures for them" (Donohue, 2010).

Virtually every parent knows of the particular issues that his or her child is having in the system. Often, those challenges are academic; sometimes they are social, sometimes emotional. School years, as we all know, can be very challenging in many ways for students, and every parent feels the pain and angst that their children go through.

What if you could paint a picture for parents of less pain and less angst for their children? What if that included improving their children's self-esteem and confidence? And, above all, what if that picture included a greater likelihood that their children would be successful and happy in their schooling, including college, and then as members of society? This is the kind of picture that can be painted for parents as we move to a competency-based, anytime, anyplace, anyhow, and any pace system. Will they have concerns? Of course. Will parents be totally convinced after one meeting? Probably not, but they should be convinced enough to continue moving forward after only one meeting if the leaders of the conversation are convincing enough for them to do so. This can only be done by someone who understands the concept well enough to give substantive answers to parents' questions and knows when to answer, "We don't yet know the answer, but we will work to learn as we go forward." Frankly, the fewer "we don't know" answers the better. For example, parents will want to know how a new system with a new reporting mechanism will impact college admissions. An "I don't know" answer will be viewed very negatively by parents and has the potential of stopping the process, including the communication with parents.

Fred recalls: On October 29, 2011, I was invited to address the community at Pittsfield, New Hampshire, High School. Pittsfield High, led by Principal Robert Bickford and Superintendent John Freeman, has been a leader in moving a competency-based system forward. At the meeting, it was evident that there were a number of skeptical, even somewhat angry parents who had many concerns and questions about the logic of moving to this new system. Many feared potentially negative ramifications for their children, especially regarding the ability to be accepted into good colleges. While the questions and comments often took on a hard and angry tone, they were addressed to the best of our ability by the principal, the superintendent, and myself. At the end of the evening, one of the most challenging parents in the group remarked that he had learned more about the direction that Pittsfield High was heading on this night than in the previous 2 to 3 years that they had been undertaking this transition. Both Principal Bickford and Superintendent Freeman remarked to me after the meeting that they felt that this gathering was very productive and that their big takeaway was communication, communication, communication. Pittsfield has had another evening similar to this one with Rose Colby.

Additionally, regarding the answer to the question of the impact of competency-based transcripts on college admissions, Fred recalls: the college admissions officers in New Hampshire have their own professional organization. My intern at the time, Jamie Richardson, a Dartmouth student, had dusted off a decade-old, competency-based transcript created by the New Hampshire Department of Education. The transcript didn't catch on when it was created in the 1990s, so the department shelved the concept. The creation of the transcript was led by department members Dr. Paul Leather, now New Hampshire's Deputy Commissioner of Education, and Mariane Gfroerer.

Jamie and I talked about what this transcript might look like with regard to the learning environment model that we were envisioning. Jamie then reworked the transcript and brought it back to me for my approval.

We then made an appointment to meet with the college admissions officers at their regularly scheduled meeting. We passed out the transcript, filled in to reflect a make-believe student who had a passion for science fiction, especially space science. The transcript showed learning in classrooms, the planetarium, online, and so forth. I then asked the admissions officers, if they had a space science program of studies at their schools, would this be the type of student they would welcome? There was an overwhelming" yes" from the group. While there were still questions to be answered, there was no sense of reluctance to accept this student.

Transformation leaders must have these kinds of meetings in order to confidently assure parents that their children will be well served and not put at a disadvantage by this new model. Frankly, they should be convinced that this model would give their students an advantage over students who have only traditional school experiences to show on their transcripts.

Other issues that parents will want to see addressed include grades, wellness, relationships with educators and peers, safety, and more. In most cases, a competency-based model will serve students better than a traditional classroom model. The following is a quick look at how a competency-based model will be better for students.

GRADES

In a competency-based, move-on-when-ready model, there should be no Ds or Fs, and a C should be a rarity. If a student must meet mastery of required competencies and he/she has yet to do so, there should be no final grade until mastery is achieved. Yet there should be many assessments along the way to building toward mastery. Grades should not be time related, although, in the early stages of redesign, many educators will try to hold on to the old model of As, Bs, Cs, Ds, and Fs on a quarterly basis.

Maintaining the elements of a time-based system will serve to corrupt the integrity of a competency-based system. Issues like homework, attendance, class participation, behavior, quizzes, and the like should play little or no role in a student's final grade. Whether the student has mastered the required competencies should be the ruling determinant. How long it takes to get there will likely be different for every student. The age-old tradition of passing students to the next level of work when they haven't mastered what they are supposed to be mastering must end. The sooner we do this, the better off our students will be.

Rose: This is a challenging area when considering that "move on when ready" throughout a child's education requires a system that supports gathering all aspects of learner growth over time and providing ready access of this information to educators throughout a child's learning history. Currently, most student information systems archive student information at the end of this school year, creating historical files on students, effectively closing out every school year. Beyond that, there are only a few student information systems that can actually track student performance by competency. It has been a difficult and expensive process for those schools that developed competency-based report cards. Tracking student performance by competency without regard to time constraints (i.e., quarters, semesters) is an area of software development that needs to be put on a fast track so that school systems have these upgrades readily available.

Spaulding High School (Rochester, New Hampshire) and the Sanborn Regional School District (New Hampshire) have adopted a rolling grade. They are fortunate to have software systems that they have customized for competency-based learning. Parents know that the grades they view on the parent portal at any point in time represent the achievement to date on essential standards or competencies. Most schools are still struggling with the software companies to associate a grade with a competency instead of recording grades by the format of the assessment (test, quiz, etc.).

Mastery is about raising the standards. Mastery is a high level of proficiency and can be achieved in more ways than sitting in a classroom. Done well, mastery should be pursued in a way that is of the students' choosing, but mastery of competencies should be the only acceptable outcome for credit and to move to the next level.

Success breeds success. If students perceive themselves in their personal, social, physical, and academic contexts as building on their individual successes and schools are doing everything possible to create and validate each learner's victories, large and small, learner confidence should build. Building a positive self-image allows the students to take increasing risks as they develop a greater level of expertise. These risks in learning are part of the learning paradigm in which students are authentic problem solvers, putting forth their ideas in collaborative ways with their peers and the adults in the learning environment. This increases expertise in learners as they seek to know more about their areas of interest. They should be encouraged to make presentations, develop websites, and create clubs—anything to bolster and validate their status as experts.

WELLNESS

The traditional approach to wellness has been for students to participate in physical education classes and to see a guidance counselor when needing to deal with other issues. In today's schools, educators understand that physical, psychological, and social factors all impact a student's wellness and learning. Substance abuse, addictive behaviors, obesity, suicide prevention, family stability, loss of family members and friends, and gang issues are all part of the world of today's learners from the entry of school until graduation. Acknowledging each of these personal challenges as part of each student's personalized learning plan can promote the learner's engagement in solving these problems using resources guided by the adults in their lives. The goal must be to find a path that is acceptable for each student to remain on a wellness plan for his/her entire life. It's highly likely that no two plans will look alike.

RELATIONSHIPS WITH ADULTS

There should be a customized/personalized plan (not an IEP) for every student. In order to put these plans together, educators will need to know who their student are—not just their names, but their interests, passions, and dreams, their strengths and weaknesses, their learning styles. Armed with this information, educators will be in a great position to help each student shape this information into a plan that will light his/her learning path. Sometimes this learning will be in classrooms, other times online, and still others in real-world environments in the community in which other adults will interact with them. There should be more adults interacting with students regarding their learning than ever before. Each adult should be aware of the appropriate information on the student's plan to help strengthen that adult–student relationship in order to focus on the student's success.

SAFETY

One question that all adults, including parents, will have is, if students, especially teenagers, aren't always in the school building at traditional times, "Is this an opportunity for getting into trouble?" Let's be clear. While students may not be scheduled to be in a school building during traditional times of the day and year, students should still have schedules. These schedules should include the times and places that students are expected to be under adult supervision as part of their learning, including their internships, work study, private instruction, sports teams, theater groups, and so forth. If students are expecting to receive credit toward graduation for choices they made beyond the school's traditional offerings, they have a responsibility to earn these credits. While credit is only granted based on a demonstration of mastery of competencies, someone in the system needs to sign off that this student has succeeded in achieving mastery. A student who has not respected the process that he/she chose may encounter human-nature difficulties in getting credit approval from the person deemed responsible for overseeing their learning experience.

Although students should have schedules that reflect where they are during times that they are engaged in formalized learning, including during nontraditional times and nontraditional environments, there will be times of the day that they may not be scheduled, just as there are times that they are not scheduled in the current system. In the old model, students are not scheduled for formalized learning after school lets out, nights, weekends, vacations, holidays, and summers. In an anytime, anyplace model, formalized learning can occur during any of these times. All in all, everyone needs to understand and accept that there will be learning times and schedules that may be different than the traditional model of school schedules. For many, these times may actually be increased—but, regardless, they will be different.

13 Selling to Business, Nonprofits, and Communities

Oftentimes, schools reach out to business, nonprofits, and the community when they are in need of sponsorship for events, resources, and partnerships for programs. In selling to business, nonprofits, and the community, a new relationship will be forged. This shift in paradigm requires deeper understanding and collaboration in developing 21st century learning.

SELLING TO BUSINESS

Educators have made overtures to businesses for decades, believing that a greater level of involvement on the part of our business community would be beneficial to students. Logically, it would seem that businesses would also want these partnerships. Unfortunately, there are a number of businesses that have tried and failed to make these partnerships succeed. All too often, the rules of school don't fit with the needs of business. The desire to engage with schools is often checked by the hassle of conforming to school structures, causing many businesses to disengage. Businesses often get frustrated having to conform to school bells/students' schedules, and so forth, resulting in fewer businesses enthusiastically willing to make these opportunities available to students.

Fred recalls: In meeting with the Lebanon, New Hampshire, business roundtable, these business leaders expressed both the desire to play a meaningful role in their schools and, simultaneously, frustration with their efforts to make it work for them. Much of the frustration was based around clocks. They complained that the students had to be back at school for period X or Y and, therefore, could not spend sufficient time at the business in order to develop a required level of expertise in order to provide a worthwhile service to the business and a worthwhile educational experience for the student. Many businesses gave up on trying to make it work. In this case, the needs of the businesses could not adequately conform to the needs of the school.

Conversely, in the Whitefield, New Hampshire, school district they developed a relationship with the Mountain View Resort to provide an internationally accepted hospitality management program for students. This program incorporated the various aspects of hospitality management, including rooms, meals, recreation, groundskeeping, building maintenance, finance, retail, and marketing. Students participated for large blocks of time, multiple days per week. Upon graduation, students were well prepared to enter the hospitality industry right out of high school or enter a college program for hospitality management.

If schools want businesses to be full partners in the process of student learning, schools need to make sure that these partnerships fit the needs of the business community and ensure that businesses see concrete benefits, not just an assuaging of their sense of altruism, but real benefits to these relationships.

The benefits to business must include the following:

- *Ease of implementation:* A serious effort must be put into clarifying the elements that would make it easy for a business to engage in this process. What are the optimal times of day when a particular business would want to engage students who want to learn the skills necessary to be employed in that industry? What is the general profile of an individual that businesses believe would be successful in their line of work? School must match students who are clearly interested in and motivated to participate in the opportunity being provided by this business. While not every student–business interaction will be a success, there clearly need to be more successes than failures. Planning by educators that helps ensure more successes will encourage businesses to maintain and foster this relationship as an ongoing part of how they function. Too many failures will discourage businesses from doing more.

- *Free labor:* Schools cannot count on sheer altruism in order to get businesses on board. Every school–business partnership needs to include a win/win perspective. This partnership should be seen as an opportunity for businesses to receive free labor in exchange for teaching students the skills necessary to succeed in the particular industry. Educators should not necessarily be framing the conversation in a "free labor" context, but the added productivity opportunity for businesses must be obvious to all. In the minds of businessmen, this benefit needs to trump the training effort that they will provide. Having their employees oversee untrained students will have a cost to it. That cost needs to be more than made up for in added productivity by the students if districts hope to engage large segments of the local business community on an ongoing basis.

Occasionally, there may even be some remuneration for students interning with businesses, especially in areas where businesses may see direct income from students under their supervision. This may include some areas in the building trades like plumbers and electricians.

- *Source of future employees:* Most companies are always looking for employees who will strengthen their business. Businesses will inevitably find some students in these internships/apprenticeships who have demonstrated the skills and attitude that the employer is seeking. It will become commonplace that companies will offer jobs to some of these interns for part-time employment or plan to offer them full-time work when the opportunity makes sense for everyone.

SELLING TO NONPROFIT ORGANIZATIONS

This will be one of the easier sell jobs. Most nonprofits' missions are education based. They have employees and members with specific skills and passions based around their missions. More often than not, they feel that they represent an underutilized community resource. More often than not, they are in near-desperate need of money. All of this makes them a near-perfect fit for a competency-based, anytime, anywhere model. The opportunity to make worthy nonprofits a virtual fixture in the public school system is, pretty much, there for the asking.

Many of these nonprofits have facilities, often with better learning environments than a school could provide for similar learning. For example, the Capitol Center for the Arts (Concord, New Hampshire) is likely to have better and more varied learning opportunities in the arts than the local schools. The Christa McAuliffe Planetarium and Alan B. Shepard Discovery

Center (Concord, New Hampshire) are much more likely to create future space scientists than high school classrooms are. Not-for-profits will represent an important part of the abundance in community resources that needs to be managed by our professional educators for the benefit of our students.

Fred recalls: The Christa McAuliffe Planetarium and Alan B. Shepard Discovery Center were very much in tune with the possibilities of what their role could become in public education, so much so that they asked me to speak on camera for their promotional video. The video can be seen at www.starhop.com.

Another New Hampshire nonprofit offering some wonderful extended learning opportunity courses to a number of school districts is the Riverbend School of Theater Arts at the Milford (New Hampshire) Boys and Girls Club led by artistic director Toby Tarnow. Toby was the first Anne in the musical version of Anne of Green Gables *(Toby Tarnow Biography, www.imdb.com).*

The benefits to the nonprofits are clear. Structured properly, they will no longer feel underutilized. They will be fulfilling their missions better than ever before and will likely create streams of revenue that they hadn't planned on. For example, if one student wanted to do an independent study at the planetarium, the planetarium might participate with no added fees, seeing that assistance as part of fulfilling their mission. If, however, 100 students wanted these services, the planetarium would likely not be able to provide those services for free. If school districts view these nonprofits as important resources, based upon student demand and the quality of the learning experience, they must now think about how to financially ensure that these resources remain an important part of their learning options. In most cases, it is likely that the nonprofits will prove to be better and more cost-effective options for districts than trying to provide similar opportunities inside of schools.

Once again, there may be fear on the part of some education groups that these nonprofits will take students away from traditional classrooms. In fact, they most likely will. As stated earlier, in the long run, only the best traditional classrooms are likely to survive as more exciting options become available to students.

SELLING TO COMMUNITIES

The communities will need to be sold on the model. Some aspects of an anytime, anyplace model will raise concerns; others will be quite appealing.

The primary concern for community members will be similar to one of the concerns of parents: "What happens when these wild teenagers are let loose with no supervision?" As stated in the "Selling Students and Parents" section, it's not that students will be unsupervised, it's that the traditional times when students were expected to be supervised are going to change. With learning opportunities no longer limited to the traditional school calendar, students may actually be under supervision more than in the past. Nights, weekends, summers, and the like will now be times when many students are working toward their credits and will be under direct supervision. However, without a doubt, some student somewhere is going to do something bad during a time when he or she would have been in school under the old system and, as a result, somebody is going to blame it on the new system. What is more likely is that as we get years of experience in an anytime, anywhere, competency-based model, we will see a reduction in crime statistics as a direct result of engaging more students.

But the major selling point to communities will be the rebuilding of community. Robert Putnam's book *Bowling Alone* (Putnam, 2001) depicts a loss of community from decades ago when our when our dads belonged to bowling leagues. Teams from all over the community were brought together to compete for league championships. But the added benefit, intended or not, was that these leagues brought together members from around the greater community who may never have met one another had it not been for bowling.

But, as time passed and American families became busier, with both parents working, and dramatic changes in the makeup of the American family (including more single-parent families, more unmarried couples with children, more divorces), the bowling leagues began to dwindle. Thus, the metaphor "bowling alone."

In an anyplace, anytime, competency-based system, public education has the potential to be the key to bringing community back. No longer will professional educators be charged with the sole responsibility to educate our students. Under this new model, the entire community will share this great responsibility with our educators, whose primary role will be coordinating the process. Businesses, nonprofits, and talented individuals will be called upon to play a larger role than ever before in the education of our students. Done well, this greater role will elevate the importance of public education in the eyes of communities and will strengthen community support for our schools. School will likely be better and less expensive, easing property tax pressures and reducing the acrimony expressed in so many districts around the country. If it is done well, virtually everybody in the community will benefit from this new model.

14 Selling to the Education Community and Professional Organizations

Just the thought of changing the nature of public education can be threatening to many educator groups. Keeping them engaged in the conversation will be both essential and challenging, especially when they understand the naturally disruptive nature of this concept to the teaching profession that they know and, in most cases, love.

SELLING TO THE EDUCATION COMMUNITY

When you mess with people's jobs, expect them to be nervous, suspicious, and skeptical, not only of yet another education reform concept but also of the motives of the individuals putting the model forward.

Fred recalls: In 2003 and 2004, I was giving presentations morning, noon, and night, trying to engage virtually any group that I could in this conversation. I knew that some groups would view this concept very favorably and that others would not. I found allies in special-needs and career and technical educators (CTE) and detractors in the arts and physical education.

The special-needs and CTE educators both believed that we had two different systems. For special education, it was the kids with plans and the kids without plans, and they hated it. They told me of the heartbreak of students with plans (IEPs), labeled, in the eyes of the students themselves, as somehow flawed and the accompanying heartbreak and damage to their psyches. The special-needs educators wanted a one-system approach in which every student has a plan—not an IEP, but a personalized/customized plan for every student based on the personalized needs, not just academic, but personal, physical, and social needs, and based on their interests, passions, dreams, and learning styles. Every student would know that every one of their peers has one of these plans and that no two are alike. A one-system approach.

The CTE educators also felt that there were two systems and they hated it. There were the students in the mainstream programs, and then there were the CTE students. They believed that the mainstream program looked down its nose at CTE, that the kids in CTE were viewed as not as smart as the students in the mainstream program. The CTE educators believed that the mainstream system had it wrong, that every student would benefit from more hands-on, more interaction in real-world offerings in the community with businesses, and so forth. They, too, wanted a one-system approach.

While the CTE and special educators were supportive of the state board's proposal, the music, arts, and physical education teachers were unhappy about the direction the board was heading. They felt that providing near-limitless options for students would threaten their programs if students saw more exciting options outside of school.

Their opposition was intensified upon the defeat of Governor Craig Benson. The music educators wrote a letter critical of my work to newly elected Governor John Lynch and his new State Board of Education Chairman and Commissioner of Education appointments.

The new state board chairman, David Ruedig, responded to their letter and invited them to meet to express their concerns. The music educators met with Chairman Ruedig at the New Hampshire Department of Education. After the meeting, Chairman Ruedig and I had a conversation. He informed me that the music educators told him that I was advocating that any student who purchased a Fender Stratocaster guitar would be able to get credit in music. Chairman Ruedig then asked if they had actually heard me speak those specific words. They responded that while they hadn't actually heard me speak those words, they believed that, in essence, is what I was saying. Chairman Ruedig told me that he responded that he has been working with me for 2 years on this topic and has never heard me state anything that resembled what they were saying. He informed me that he believed they weren't very satisfied with the meeting.

Not long thereafter, at the New Hampshire Excellence in Education Awards (the Edies), a gala event at which I was the master of ceremonies, the music educators were called to the stage to receive the Music Educator of the Year award. I warmly greeted their recipient, who may well have been one of the members who met with Chairman Ruedig. At the dinner break, I went over to their table and said, "We need to talk." They agreed.

Subsequently, their president, Pat Anderson, and I met for lunch. Pat suggested that I speak to the music educators at their Oktoberfest meeting in the fall. I accepted but asked to make two presentations, one to the music educators and a second meeting with members of the music community and music educators together. She agreed.

At the event, in the first meeting, a number of New Hampshire music educators packed the room while members of the music community sat in the audience to listen to the conversation. The meeting was intense, with a fair amount of spit flying and teeth gnashing. I was being accused of threatening music programs all over the state. People feared that, given options, many students would leave current music programs. I explained that, as someone who earns a living selling music products, I had no desire to anger the state's music educators. My interest was to engage more learners through their love of music, to create more music makers, to broaden students' participation in making music, and to allow those students to receive music credit for a measured and successful music experience regardless of where, when, or how that participation occurred. We went back and forth until one of the members of the music community spoke up.

TJ Wheeler, New Hampshire's premier blues educator, a past national winner of the W.C. Handy Award, asked if he could address the group. He told the group that our "discussion" reminded him of postreconstruction New Orleans.

TJ talked about changes caused by the Jim Crow laws. He spoke of how New Orleans was the most racially diverse city in America—so diverse that names like octoroon, quadroon, mulatto, and more referred to these mixed-race groups.

He explained that the lighter-skinned groups enjoyed more privileges than those with darker skin and that the African blacks had the fewest privileges of all, including their education, jobs, and housing. This changed with the Jim Crow laws. These laws included what was known as the one-drop rule: Anyone with one drop of black blood was now considered to be black. All of a sudden, like it or not, these groups were thrown together into the same poor circumstances as the blacks.

(Continued)

(Continued)

Prior to the Jim Crow laws, musicians among the lighter-skinned groups studied European masters. The African blacks were the street musicians, carrying over musical traditions from their homeland. Since they were now living together, their musicians started playing together, and the result was the birth of jazz.

The key points of TJ Wheeler's analogy include:

- *For reasons of self-interest, those who are satisfied with what they are doing won't want things to change. It will take skilled leadership to ensure that the concept is not compromised for adults' interests, therefore slowing education's move into the 21st century.*
- *Whether or not all educators are happy with outside groups and individuals now having the opportunity to play a significant role in what they may have viewed as "their turf," the potential from combining the dedication of our professional educators with their contemporaries in the community at large has the potential of creating something as special as jazz.*

(The full text of TJ Wheeler's comments can be found in the Appendix.)

EASING THE UNEASY

Selling groups or individuals on a concept that they see as disruptive or even threatening to their jobs will not be easy. A conscious effort must be made to assure educators that this transition to an anytime, anyplace model will not be a flip of a switch, that it will take a period of years and will constantly evolve. They must also be assured that the school will be supportive of professional development efforts to assist educators as the school, district, and state in acquiring more experience in moving to the new model, and, most importantly, that we will learn together as we move forward with the new model.

There has always been reluctance at the high school level to step out of the traditional box because of the perception that accrediting agencies, colleges, and universities will not be accepting of new or different models of high school learning. Colleges and universities currently accept students who have graduated both from traditional programs and from many other preparatory experiences. Home-school students, International Baccalaureate students, graduates of charter schools, graduates from secondary schools who present portfolios, and international students have all found admission in our colleges and universities. Parents of high school students often don't understand the diverse nature of admissions into postsecondary schools. They hold on to many old customs, thinking that to do otherwise would hinder their child's admission. One such belief is that class rank must be used in the college admission process. Because of the diversity of applicants to colleges from many different high school settings, class rank does not hold the sway it has in the past. To that end, many high schools have abandoned the valedictorian system of honoring scholars to the recognition of summa cum laude, magna cum laude, and cum laude scholars in a graduating class.

Rose: In working with many high schools in developing competency-based grading systems, I have found that oftentimes, parents are the most reluctant in abandoning elements of traditional grading because of the notion that any new grading system may hurt their child's opportunity to gain admission to college. When moving to competency-based grading systems, we have noted that grade deflation does occur. Another notable observation is that more students are successful in passing courses because of the need to relearn and reassess when needed. Lebanon High School chose to gradually change the school culture for grading. They introduced competency-based grading as students entered high school. The first year, ninth-grade students were graded using the new grading philosophy. The following year, tenth-grade teachers used the new grading philosophy. Phasing in competency-based grading provided professional development time and opportunity for the staff to create the needed competency-based learning framework of designing high-quality competencies, performance indicators, and assessment systems. Schools that introduced competency-based grading for all students in Grades 9 through 12 at the same time experienced difficulty in communicating to parents and students the sudden change in culture.

The New England Association of Schools and Colleges (N.E.A.S.C.) was involved early on in the conversations surrounding the development of competencies in New Hampshire. N.E.A.S.C.'s standards for accreditation were not problematic for schools that were developing competency-based learning systems that included extended learning opportunities.

AN ENDORSEMENT FROM A TEACHER WHO COULD BE YOU

The future holds as many hopeful expectations as it does anxieties for the practitioner. Might this be a reflection of an experienced teacher who transformed from the 20th century model to the 21st century model of teaching and learning?

I've been teaching for 23 years and was considering retirement. Yes, I still like teaching, but it had gotten somewhat old to me. I've taught these lessons so many times that I could teach my classes with my eyes closed and hands behind my back. Five teaching periods per day, five days a week. Same subjects, different kids, year after year. Burned out? I wouldn't call it that—more bored than anything else.

But then it all changed. At first I thought, "Here we go again, yet another education reform concept. Real World Learning, competency-based learning? (Yawn). Ya, right! Just tell me what I'm supposed to do." Between you and me, I was just going to fit it in to what I have always done just like I have with all of the other, so called, reforms that I've seen come and go.

Boy, was I wrong. Although my major was biology, I've always loved all of the sciences. Since moving to a competency-based, anytime, anywhere system, you can't believe what my day is like. I teach only two classes per day, three days per week, to students who have specifically requested to have me teach them. I've always had a number of these kids in my classes but they were spread out over five classes and five days. Now I have classes packed with students who really want to be there. These kids are excited about coming to my class. To have them grouped together is challenging and energizing: These classes are full of students who remind me of my enthusiasm for science when I was their age.

I have another class of independent science study. I supervise 20–25 kids with laptops. Each student is studying some aspect of science through online courses that they have chosen. After these students researched various online courses that they were considering, I counseled them about various options and I helped them move, thoughtfully, through them. Some are studying rainforests; others are studying oceanography, wetland habitats, seismology, and many other subjects. These kids are picking their courses for great reasons. Some of them talk about careers in these areas. There are virtually zero discipline issues.

Of these independent studies, I'm assisting in 18 different course offerings. We could never have provided this level of study to our students, and every one of these kids is seriously into their work. In the process, I'm learning more than I ever dreamed, including about subjects that I had modest expertise in. There are seven kids in this school studying various aspects of the rainforest. Another teacher and I are investigating taking a summer trip for two weeks to Costa Rica with these students. They'll be earning credit toward graduation for Advanced Rainforest Studies.

At 1:00 today, I have two people from Lonza Biologics, a science research company, coming over to talk about taking on interns for credit. This will be a great opportunity for interested students to do hands on work with real scientists. We need to discuss the nature of the students' experience, each party's goals for this effort, the number of students, time requirements and school oversight. I'm looking forward to going over to see their facilities.

I spend more of my time doing research than ever, meeting with members of the science community in my area, looking for opportunities for my students. I meet students in small groups or individually, counseling them and going over their work. My day is so varied.

Today, at 3:00 I'll go over to the Jackson Oceanography Lab at UNH. I have two students interning with Dr. Watson in marine biology. Did you know that lobsters actually go in and out of lobster traps whenever they want? I'm being more productive than ever. I'm learning more than ever. Retire? Forget it. I'm having way too much fun.

Dr. Leo Corriveau, former executive director for the College of Graduate Studies at Plymouth (New Hampshire) State University and now superintendent of school for the Mascenic (New Hampshire) School District, advises, "It's all about relationships." Do you have the personal skills to be able to paint the picture for your professional educators that will have them trusting enough to engage in a conversation about moving toward a model that they were not trained for? One that could threaten the nature of how they perform their duties? Painting that picture of what jobs could look like in the new delivery model is critical to reducing anxieties about what their future role will be.

Rose: We are asking educators to work in ways the system to date has not supported on many different levels. In many conversations with teachers, they acknowledge that moving to a new model is intriguing and energizing, but they fear that innovation in their classrooms will bring on problems from their administrators. Some of these educators are the walking wounded. They tried some innovative or creative efforts but, when confronted with parental pressure, found their school leaders did not support them. Developing strong school leader–educator relationships should be part of school change efforts. School leaders need to pay attention to the quality of the work environment for the adults in the school environment, especially when educators are introducing new approaches and pedagogy. Creating positive relationships between leaders and educators is essential.

SELLING TO PROFESSIONAL ORGANIZATIONS

In abandoning the traditional system of moving students along by age-based grades, local school leaders, teachers, and parents need to look at their school facilities, learning resources, and professional and paraprofessional staff quite differently. School leaders and teachers who have been involved with introducing Response to Intervention programs can attest that you have to first look at the desired outcome and redesign resources around that to reach the desired results. Trying to fit new systems into old schedules doesn't generally work well. Overcoming these challenges requires leaders who are impassioned by the vision and capable of influencing reluctant educators, parents, and community members. Professional organizations that support principals, associate principals, curriculum coordinators, special educators, and teachers will have to refashion themselves to this new paradigm to provide expertise and coaching to their members, or their roles may soon be obsolete.

Rose: In New Hampshire, the New Hampshire Association of School Principals (N.H.A.S.P.) and the New Hampshire School Administrators Association (N.H.S.A.A.) provided ongoing support to school leaders through the transition to competency development at the secondary level. Both organizations supported their membership with meaningful opportunities to learn and lead their school organizations. N.H.A.S.P. provided regularly scheduled regional evening network meetings for high school principals to discuss the various aspects of moving to competencies. Having a focused conversation over dinner developed strong professional associations over time.

15 Selling the Concept and the Politics to Legislators

Building political capital necessary to gain approval of substantive school redesign around anytime, anyplace, anyhow, any pace, competency-based mastery learning is a formidable task but a necessary one. It is necessary to bring these stakeholders into the process early on by having each member of the redesign group partner with local and state representatives. Keeping the political arm of this effort both engaged and informed can speed up the required regulatory processes. It is very important to partner with legislators and local government officials, especially those who, at the outset, may not be seen as friendly to public education.

Some might prefer that this book stay away from politics. Unfortunately, separating education from politics is impossible. Politics will play an important role in making this transition. While the concept itself is apolitical, those charged with the enormous task of transforming education need to think in political terms. Not Republican terms . . . not Democratic terms . . . but both. They need to understand how to speak the language of both parties and be convincing. This is not an easy task and requires politically savvy individuals to successfully navigate these waters.

Fred recalls: As chairman of the State Board of Education, I met with members of the Joint Legislative Committee on Administrative Rules (JLCAR) on numerous occasions. These were state senators and members of New Hampshire's House of Representatives who were going to have a significant impact on whether these rules would pass. Yes, there were negotiations. Sometimes I had to give up on things I wanted in order to move the larger concept forward. I cannot emphasize enough that the relationship part of making monumental change does not happen by luck. As Dr. Leo Corriveau has often stated to me, "It's all about relationships."

During this period, I was investing approximately 50 hours per week on school redesign. It is my sense that very few colleagues from around the country in similar positions are able to put in such a similarly focused effort for no pay. Fortunately for me and for New Hampshire, our state is small, and my paying job allowed me the flexibility to use my time to meet with virtually every stakeholder group in the process, including our legislators. I met regularly with House education Chairman Steve L'Heureux (R), who later became a colleague on the New Hampshire State Board of Education. In all likelihood, states will need to form teams, probably led by their departments of education, state boards, and school administrators. Utilizing resources such as this book and the work of the Counsel of Chief State School Officers, the Nellie Mae Education Foundation, the Stupski Foundation, CESA #1 in Wisconsin, and the work of Susan Patrick (iNACOL) and Chris Sturgis (Medisnet) will be extremely helpful in training state teams to be sufficiently conversant in selling the concept to all groups, including policymakers.

SELLING A NONPARTISAN CONCEPT TO PARTISANS

Like it or not, education is very political. Trying to make it nonpolitical is an admirable goal, one for which every school board should strive. Good luck, because it's easier said than done. So much of this is about individuals' personal styles. Combative personalities make for political problems. It's not that school boards have to be full of pussycats. It's that, unfortunately, all too often, firebrands get elected for the purpose of breathing fire.

Fred recalls: When I was first appointed to the state board (1992), all seven members were appointed by then-Governor Judd Gregg. The political persuasions of the board members ranged from moderate to very conservative. The conservatives, including then-board chair Judith Thayer, were pushing their agenda. While the agenda had merit, the methodology, which felt to the education community to be too heavy handed, did not go over well and caused an enormous backlash. The board lost a great deal of respect in the education community.

In 2003, when I was asked to chair the board by newly elected Governor Craig Benson (R), the other six board members had been appointed by his predecessor, Governor Jeanne Shaheen (D). I was the only Benson appointee and, oftentimes, you could feel the tension. Governor Benson did not have friends on this board— that is, besides me.

As board terms expired, Governor Benson replaced board members with his appointees. I would bring the governor the names of strong individuals who I felt would be solid board members and who also would not bring a volatile political agenda. Governor Benson appointed New Hampshire's first African American to the State Board of Education, an independent, Bill Walker, the director of minority health at the New Hampshire Department of Health and Human Services. He appointed Mary McNeil, a Democrat, who went on to head the education department at Rivier College. With the varied backgrounds and mild-mannered personalities of Governor Benson's appointees, the political tensions began to dissipate.

Governor Lynch (D) has followed that same tradition. Currently, the membership of the New Hampshire state board, all appointed by Governor Lynch, is made up of three Republicans, three Democrats, and one independent. We function as a team that places the best interests of students as our top priority. I recognize that, while the pace of change is too slow for me, we may be moving at a faster pace than any other state board of education in the country. While my "pleasant pain in the neck" personality sometimes drives my fellow board members and Department of Education personnel crazy, as I push harder for redesign, I appreciate how lucky I am to serve with this great group of individuals. I am convinced that audience members at New Hampshire state board meetings would have a difficult time discerning the political persuasions of the individual members of our board. Hopefully, it will stay that way.

A competency-based agenda is not a political agenda. It has much to love by all political persuasions. I have given nearly 1,000 presentations since 2003 on this subject to groups from all over the political spectrum and have not gotten a lot of pushback. Frankly, I especially love talking to conservative groups about a new model of public education. They generally start the meeting very skeptical and end up convinced. We are making progress as a result of keeping the politics at bay and shining light on the great benefits of this new system to virtually every stakeholder group.

Off the Clock Selling Points for Democrats

- We are creating a 21st century system of public education that will strengthen public education for the foreseeable future.
- It will be more public than ever before by harnessing the resources of the entire community.

- It will bring back a greater sense of community for the well-being of everyone, especially our students.
- It will offer educational opportunities that the entire community can participate in.
- It will reduce acrimony over school issues, especially around money.
- It will reduce costs without sacrificing quality.
- It will strengthen community businesses and not-for-profits.
- It will create better futures for our students than ever before.
- It can save enough money in high schools to begin to consider options like preschool and early college.
- It can make college more affordable.

Concerns for Democrats

Q: Will this be threatening to teachers' jobs?

A: While it is threatening to 20th century roles, it's opening up 21st century educator positions.

In 2008, the Mascenic (New Hampshire) School District advertised for the position of Spanish teacher. When the interviews with the candidates were completed, the review team contacted Superintendent Dr. Leo Corriveau for the purpose of offering the job to the top candidate. When Superintendent Corriveau sat down with the young lady, he said to her that they would offer her the job and that she would teach Spanish, but her real job would be the foreign language coordinator; they were going to bring in a number of Rosetta Stone courses and she would oversee their usage. She responded, "Great!"

This is just one example of how, because of technology and the competency-based model, a foreign language teacher becomes the foreign language coordinator, overseeing students who are learning a variety of languages.

Off the Clock Selling Points for Republicans

- Students and parents will have more control over the education process than ever before.
- The system will be market driven based on student demand.
- It will make obsolete past sacred cows like seniority- and time-based compensation models.
- It will provide more choices for students and parents than ever before.
- It will make better opportunities available to students for less cost than the current system.

- Some nontraditional outside credit-bearing choices will be paid for by parents/students (i.e., private music lessons).
- It will provide a source of future employees to local businesses.

Concerns for Republicans

Q: Is this competency-based education a new version of the outcomes-based education concept of the 1990s?

A: The outcomes-based concept of the 1990s was characterized, rightly or wrongly, as a left-wing takeover of public of education. There were fears that our students would be brainwashed with revisionist history lessons that would portray many American heroes as bad guys, that it would take away any hope of accountability, and other claims guaranteed to send chills up the spines of conservatives. Those concerns from the past have absolutely nothing to do with the work done in New Hampshire. The New Hampshire model was initiated under a conservative Republican governor and a Republican chair of the state board of education. Conservatives characterized the concept as "homeschooling with professional oversight." It is surviving and growing under a Democratic governor.

The concept itself is apolitical. Leaders must have the skills and knowledge to douse the potential fires created by partisans on either the left or the right to prevent politicizing a system that offers great benefits.

Part V

Imagine the Possibilities

Moving our system of education from its time-based anchor in the past is a formidable task. It is important to keep a sharp focus on the vision of the future with all of its possibilities, its challenges, and its rewards for all stakeholders.

16 Moving Education From Time to Competency

The significance of the changes made by the New Hampshire Board of Education to its school approval rules has the potential to change the role of public education, not only in New Hampshire but also starting a process that will spread across America. Already, the concept of a competency-based system has become a front-burner issue for the Council of Chief State School Officers (CCSSO), and New Hampshire appears to be its poster child.

To casual observers of the changes being made in New Hampshire, the significance is not likely to be as jaw dropping as it would be if observers were to understand their potential collective ramifications. While the New Hampshire board could not have been more public and open with the process of gathering input on proposed rule changes, it seems that very few have actually taken the time to contemplate the collective impact these rules will have on the traditional public education delivery model.

Feeling fully confident that the impact will be positive, the possible ramifications on our professional staff may be more than some would want and are prepared for. With this new model for learning, many jobs will change. Some will go away. Others will be added, and our students will be the primary beneficiaries.

SEISMIC CHANGE

- Schools will change their focus from all students to each student.
- Control over how students are educated will move away from system control to a shared responsibility among the system, the parents, and, most importantly, the students themselves.
- Teachers' primary role will move away from full-time direct delivery of content in classrooms and will move toward that of facilitators, coaches, mentors, and guides; they will provide quality control, inspiration, motivation, guidance, and advocacy.
- Some teachers may no longer be full-time employees of a single school district but may work for multiple districts.
- The concept of high school itself will move away from a physical plant and toward the experience of learning.
- A steadily decreasing percentage of learning will be done in traditional classroom settings, resulting in fewer students in buildings and reduced pressure on school construction.
- Teacher compensation will move from a time-based model to a performance-based model.
- Curriculum offerings will no longer be limited to the courses within the building but will become virtually limitless by harnessing the available resources in communities and through technology.
- Learning will move away from curriculum silos and toward interdisciplinary, project-based learning.
- Education will no longer be viewed as 9½ months but as an uninterrupted, lifelong experience.
- Credit will no longer be based on seat time but on student mastery of required competencies.
- Day One will no longer begin with page one, chapter one, but will begin with a concerted effort to understand the personal needs, passions, interests, and learning styles of each student.
- Each student will have a plan—not an IEP, but a personalized learning plan, which the student will develop in collaboration with teachers and parents. This plan will be a dynamic tool in shaping each student's pathway for learning.
- The dropout rate will be virtually eliminated, as every student will be an engaged learner. The word *boring* will no longer be synonymous with *school*.
- Public education will be vastly better, more efficient, and, quite possibly, less expensive.

LIMITLESS LEARNING OPPORTUNITIES

Envision a school calendar that accepted flexibility as the norm, that students (especially high school students) are not all expected to be in the building for set periods of time, but could be at home taking an online course, serving as an apprentice with a sculptor, working as an intern at a local auto dealership, taking private piano lessons, or living with a French family in Paris and learning to speak French. All of this and endless further possibilities will exist for credit toward graduation.

Envision the opportunities for foreign language credit alone. Currently, most high schools offer French and Spanish. Under the new structure, all languages would be possible. There are online courses for virtually any language. In addition to the online offerings, real-world opportunities—through travel or tutoring in your community by individuals willing to teach Chinese, Russian, Japanese, Farsi, Greek, Albanian, Italian, and so forth—will make language learning nearly limitless.

Now take that same thinking to other courses. For science, options will no longer be limited to chemistry, physics, biology, and earth science classes. They will now include virtually every science course of study you can imagine: quark theory, flight, sharks, and forestry. And who's doing the teaching? The Audubon Society, the planetarium, the air traffic control tower, science-related businesses such as Lonza Biologics and Fischer Scientific, retired scientists, online and distance learning courses, and more in collaboration with a learner's team of educators. Again, endless possibilities.

New Hampshire high schools are required to offer three units of art (see New Hampshire School Approval Rules 306–1). These units have always been thought of as courses within the walls of the building. With the new rules, the opportunities in every subject area could go from 3 to 30 or 300!! Many students are already engaged in activities that could fulfill the art requirements totally outside of the traditional classroom through the school band, private instrument lessons, church choir, playing in a rock band, performing in a theatrical troupe, and the like. For these students, the teacher's primary job may no longer be direct classroom delivery but guidance and quality-control oversight to ensure that outside experiences are rigorous and worthy of credit.

The job of the art teacher may transition from teaching five periods per day, 5 days a week to teaching only two periods a day and mentoring students, overseeing their progress, and working with local arts organizations, businesses, or talented individuals as a regular part of their daily function. Frankly, it's likely to be a more exciting and rewarding job.

But it could change even more than that. Schools will put together arts councils made up of volunteers from the community, and their primary function will be to seek out and vet the various arts assets in their region, including finding individuals who would want to be involved in arts education. Many of these opportunities will prove to be exciting to students, will become significant to the school's offerings, and will be delivered by talented individuals who have the potential to be certified as educators through an existing or future alternative certification path and, as a result, will require less direct school supervision. Think of how many of these individuals and organizations you are aware of in your community. Then imagine how many of these untapped assets you are not aware of and how many would come out of the woodwork if the opportunity to become important to public education presented itself, especially if it included the possibility of personal financial benefits.

Is it possible that there are curriculum areas such as the arts, that, in some districts, would no longer exist in traditional classrooms. Is that a good thing or a bad thing? Could arts teachers transition to becoming full-time arts coordinators? Possibly, but there would likely have to be a strong arts presence in the community to ensure quality offerings for our students. Arts educators have been living in fear of programs being cut for decades and are likely to have their concerns raised at the thought of these nontraditional offerings eliminating the need for traditional art classes. There needs to be constant vigilance by the entire arts community along with parents and students to ensure that the opportunities presented by this new model do not get abused into allowing marginal offerings to be used to cut arts programs in order to address budgetary concerns. Ensuring quality offerings in the arts or any other curriculum area must be at the forefront of every nontraditional decision.

Let's think about social studies. Internships with local governing bodies, social services groups, or political candidates, involvement with causes such as Save the Whales, women's rights, and Free Tibet: There are virtually endless opportunities that are certain to engender the passions of virtually every student.

While many of these opportunities have the potential to be life-changing experiences for students, many of them will still require the oversight of highly skilled, district-employed educators to ensure that the desired lessons and skills are learned. Experiences such as these might have educators interacting with small groups of students, with individuals, or in traditional classroom settings for part of the experience.

ISSUES AROUND RESOURCES

But who pays for all of these experiences? The schools are likely to still have a number of traditional offerings within the school walls. They will be available to every student, free as always. Although some of the options, like private instrument lessons, could be available for credit, they are options and, if chosen by students, are likely to continue to be paid for by the student and/or his/her parents. Some online course options are also likely to be paid for by the student/family.

What about those students whose families cannot afford private lessons or online courses? Options should be available to every student, and districts should make significant efforts to ensure that students from disadvantaged families have access to a variety of offerings outside of the traditional classroom. Although a district is not likely to pay for poorer students to go to France for the summer to learn to speak French, the money-saving aspects of this new model should ensure that options like online courses, private lessons, and so on can be made available to students who cannot afford costs that may be attached to some outside options.

Additionally, although most states continue to wrestle with education funding, most legislatures have been consistent in channeling added funding to districts with needy students, including special education, free and reduced-fee lunches, and English language learners. Even though these dollars are often attached to specific students and move with those students when they move from district to district, for the most part, these monies end up being comingled and used at the discretion of the district's leadership. Although districts have not commonly used those funds for individual students, it is conceivable that districts could consider using some of this money to "follow the child" to ensure that experiences beyond the classroom, referred to as extended learning opportunities (ELOs), are available for each student and that many wonderful opportunities do not become about the "haves" and "have nots."

Fortunately, many of the resources needed to make a true competency-based system a reality are already in place in our communities and, through technology, come with little or no cost. In most cases, those resources are far better than those available inside the walls of our public schools. The auto dealership is likely to have far better, more up-to-date resources than a school's auto tech program. The planetarium is likely to have far better resources to teach space exploration than a science classroom. All of these resources can be harnessed to benefit our students. A major component of public education's new role will be to make sure that these community assets and resources are found and properly managed.

Some of these resources that a district finds valuable to its mission of engaging every student will have costs associated with them (i.e., private piano lessons). If so, schools must think about how to make the money components work. A key to how successful our students will be depends on our schools being adept in understanding the needs of each partner and working diligently to ensure that all parties benefit from this effort.

If, of the 1,000 students in your school, approximately half are engaged in learning both in and outside of the school and online, and only half are in the building at any particular time, the pressure to constantly build facilities will be reduced. It is possible that this model could address many of the other seemingly endless costs of public education. Here are some cost-saving benefits of this new model:

1. Reduced pressure to build facilities

2. Minimize duplication of student effort. A personalized learning plan that defines competencies required for graduation will guide the learner along the path in making choices for study. Using such a holistic approach, there will be less overlap of content and student effort.

3. The potential for fewer full-time district employees

4. The full engagement of the community resources (i.e., organizations, businesses, and talented individuals) at a lower cost than direct classroom delivery

5. Parents paying for credit options like private music lessons

6. Many will be able to complete their high school requirements in less than 4 years.
   - Summers, nights, and weekends will be productive learning time for students to earn credit toward graduation.
   - Middle school students will be able to receive high school credit for passing high school courses.

7. Options in the school calendar could have cost-savings implications (i.e., 4-day weeks in winters to save fuel).

8. When students move forward in their learning based on their ability to demonstrate mastery of competencies, the cost of retention, credit recovery, and other interventions will be reduced.

While the potential for cost savings is significant, there are areas that are likely to have cost implications, including:

1. Addressing equity issues to ensure that opportunities are available to students whose families cannot afford to pay for private lessons, tutoring, and the like.

2. A customized plan enabling students to own their learning will result in the virtual elimination of dropouts, meaning more students enrolled in the system.

3. With savings in other areas, there will be pressure to address other issues.

   - Unaddressed past district wants will be considered (i.e., pre-school, full-day kindergarten, updated athletic facilities).
   - Early college options will be considered, giving students the potential to finish plus or minus 2 years of college while in high school.

   The savings to students and families can be substantial.

   - More time spent with students who are of the highest need in various areas (i.e., reading, obesity, etc.)

4. Professional development/teacher training; may have associated costs during the transition to the new model

5. Many home-schooled students and students in private schools will be lured back to public education.

Rose: Several New Hampshire high schools have restructured their summer school credit-recovery programs by having students engage in relearning and demonstrating mastery only for those competencies they have yet to master. The summer session is over when the student demonstrates mastery of those competencies.

WHO'S IN CONTROL?

Who will be in control of all of this? Certainly, the school board and school administrators will still have significant control, but not as much as they now have. When this new model is adopted, many of our school leaders will want to ensure that their management methodologies are not disrupted. Conversely, this model is designed to ensure that significant power will be shifted to enable students and their parents to have a much more significant role in shaping each student's education path than they currently have.

When personalized learning plans are combined with ELOs that allow students to bring forward proposals to meet school requirements outside of the traditional classrooms, the school will have limited ability to say "no."

Fred recalls: A student came before the New Hampshire State Board of Education to tell of her experience. She passed two online Advanced Placement language arts courses through Johns Hopkins University. She informed us that colleges all over the country would accept these courses as meeting their requirements toward admission, yet her high school said "no." She calculated that she would have had to spend 48,600 minutes in class and homework assignments, learning what she already knows, in order to meet her school's requirements.

Under the new rules, every student has the option of bringing forth proposals for ELOs and to demonstrate mastery of required competencies in order to achieve course credit. A course offering from Johns Hopkins is likely to be a very credible option and, if she could pass those courses, she most likely can demonstrate mastery of the competencies. If the school said "no," under New Hampshire's new regulations, in cases like this one, the school would be putting itself in a position for a challenge that could go to the state board of education. While districts will be able to develop their own policies regarding how they will address issues such as this, those policies need to meet the spirit of the regulations. In New Hampshire, there is only one way to receive credit toward graduation. That is a demonstration of mastery of the required competencies. If a student can demonstrate that mastery, it is likely that the State Board would side with the student. The best advice for all parties is to use common sense, be reasonable, work in the best interests of each student, and not attempt to protect an outdated school model.

CAN YOU SEE IT?

The authors hope that after you have read this book, the picture of the new model of public education has become clearer to you. We also hope that this model looks better to you than the old model and that you will commit to playing a role in creating this system in your district. Yes, there will be obstacles, but hopefully, you are better prepared to work to overcome them. What can you do now? What will you do?

Appendix

COMPETENCIES

Competency Validation Tool and Technical Advisory (http://www.education .nh.gov/innovations/hs_redesign/competencies.htm)

COMPETENCY-BASED LEARNING

Sturgis, C., & Patrick, S. (2010). *When success is the only option: Designing competency based pathways for next generation learning.* Vienna, VA: International Association for K-12 Online Learning.

iNACOL (http://www.inacol.org/research/competency/index.php)

iNACOL Competency-Based Pathways Wiki (https://sites.google.com/site/competencybasedpathways/)

Sanborn Regional School District Teacher Reflection video on K–12 Standards/Competency 2010–11 Redesign (http://youtu.be/6Ps2gEKUYfE)

COMPETENCY-BASED LEARNING GRADING PHILOSOPHY STATEMENTS

Newfound Regional High School, Bristol, NH (https://sites.google.com/a/sau4.org/nrhs/report-card)

Sanborn Regional High School, Kingston, NH (http://web.sau17.org/schools/high-school/196-faculty-handbook)

Spaulding High School, Rochester, NH (https://sites.google.com/site/newtoshsfaq/home/competency-instructional-system)

EXTENDED LEARNING OPPORTUNITIES

Freeley, M. E., & Hanzelka, R. (2009). Getting away from seat time: A New Hampshire initiative encourages schools to move toward competency-based learning. *Educational Leadership, 67*(3), 63–67.

New Hampshire Resource information (http://www.education.nh.gov/innovations/elo/index.htm)

UMass Donahue Institute. (2011). New Hampshire extended learning opportunities. Final report of evaluation findings. Hadley, MA: Author.

GRADING

Guskey, T. R. (2008). Practical solutions for serious problems in standards-based grading. Thousand Oaks, CA: Corwin.
Guskey, T. R., & Bailey, M. J. M. (2009). Developing standards-based report cards. Thousand Oaks, CA: Corwin.
Marzano, R. J. (2006). Classroom assessment & grading that work. Alexandria, VA: Association for Supervision & Curriculum Development.
O'Connor, K. (2009). How to grade for learning, K–12. Thousand Oaks, CA: Corwin.
Wormeli, R. (2006). Fair isn't always equal. Portland, ME: Stenhouse Publishers.

NEW HAMPSHIRE VISION FOR HIGH SCHOOL REDESIGN

http://www.education.nh.gov/innovations/hs_redesign/index.htm

Following is a transcript of TJ Wheeler's address at the 2004 New Hampshire Music Education Octoberfest:

> Well over a 100 years ago, in the city of New Orleans, the post reconstruction Jim Crow laws ended an unfair, but unique, system of racial divisions and replaced them with another unfair system of racial division. Previously, as opposed to the rest of the slave states, a several tier racial hierarchy existed. Simply put, if you were African American, the lighter skin you were the more rights and opportunities you would have. This included what areas you lived in, job preference and education. A few of the division labels were Octoroon, Quadroon & Mulatto, or, the more generalized term of Creole (which often could be a blend of African, French, Spanish, and Native American). There was still discrimination, but less for the ones who resembled the ruling class/race.

Jim Crow changed all of this. New Orleanians had to conform closer to the "One Drop law," which meant anyone, with even the slightest ancestry of African heritage, no matter how light, would be regarded as "Negro."

This meant that lighter skin African Americans now were, like it or not, forced to live with the same amount of racial discrimination as the blackest members of their community.

In the Creole community, which was accustomed to having more rights, the new laws were generally not taken well. The overall New Orleans musical community was affected as well. Creole musicians, who had had the benefit of studying musical theory, and the harmonic concepts of the European Classical masters, were now dwelling and mixing musically and otherwise with what formerly had been decreed as a lower class of musicians, let alone people.

These so called "lower class Negro musicians" were actually descendants of Africans who for generations, during slavery, had proudly kept their African music heritage alive. On Sundays they were allowed to perform traditional African drumming and dancing in a place they called Congo Square (which is historically marked and located in Louis Armstrong Park in the perimeter of the French Quarter). Everywhere else in slave states, because of their power to send messages and instill positive retention of African culture, African Drumming had been banned.

After the Civil War, a deluge of cheap brass and percussion instruments, left over from the Confederate Army marching bands, wound up in the metropolitan city of New Orleans. Many African Americans, of all classes, suddenly had a new musical resource. The darker skin musicians integrated the new instruments with the African polyurethanes drumming of Congo Square.

Despite the cultural clash within the African American community, caused by the new Jim Crow laws, an interesting alchemy occurred. Creole musicians were suddenly playing with dark skin musicians. Social class issues aside, the mixture of these groups forged together, exchanging knowledge and blending styles ranging from Classical and Ragtime to the Blues, created the biggest revolutionary musical force of the 20th century. It has been lauded, world wide, as America's greatest gift to the Arts and Music Science. Through Duke Ellington preferred to call it African American Classical Music . . . the world for over a 100 years has simply called it JAZZ.

Bibliography

Benson, C. (2003, January 9). *Inaugural address*. New Hampshire State House, Concord, NH.

Bransford, J. D., Brown, A. L., & Cocking, R. R. (1999). *How people learn: Brain, mind, experience, and school*. Washington, DC: National Academy Press.

Brown, D. (2010). *An open letter to educators*. www.youtube.com/watch?v=.P2P GGeTOA4

Carroll, T. (2010, May 26). *The national imperative to transform educator development, schooling and the role of teachers*. New Hampshire Summit on Redefining Educator Development for 21st Century Learners. Southern New Hampshire University, Manchester, NH. http://avstream.snhu.edu:8134/videoplayer .html?source=rtmp:/publicvids/Tom%20Carroll.flv

Council of Chief State School Officers. (2011). *InTASC model core teaching standards: A resource for state dialogue*. Washington, DC: Author. http://www.ccsso.org/ Resources/Publications/InTASC_Model_Core_Teaching_Standards_A_ Resource_for_State_Dialogue_%28April_2011%29.html

Donohue, N. (2010, May 26). *Closing address*. New Hampshire Summit on Redefining Educator Development for 21st Century Learners. Southern New Hampshire University, Manchester, NH. http://www.education.nh.gov/ innovations/challenges-video.htm

Fairchild, R., Smink, J., & Steward, A. (2009). *It's time for summer: An analysis of recent policy and funding opportunities*. New York: Wallace Foundation.

Gates, B. (2005, February 26). *Prepared remarks*. Keynote address to the National Commission on High School Dropouts, Washington, DC.

Guggenheim, Davis, producer. (2011). *Waiting for Superman* (DVD, Video).

Guskey, T. R. (2008). *Practical solutions for serious problems in standards-based grading*. Thousand Oaks, CA: Corwin.

Guskey, T. R., & Bailey, M. J. M. (2009). *Developing standards-based report cards*. Thousand Oaks, CA: Corwin.

Hall, D. E. (2003). *One in four: School drop-outs in New Hampshire*. Concord, NH: New Hampshire Center for Public Policy Studies. www.NHpolicy.org/reports/ dropouts.pdf

iNACOL. (2011). *Fast facts about online learning*. Vienna, VA: Author. http://www .google.com/url?sa=t&rct=j&q=&esrc=s&source=web&cd=1&ved=0CEEQFj AA&url=http%3A%2F%2Fwww.inacol.org%2Fpress%2Fnacol_fast_facts.pdf

&ei=zCwPT4u5NOHi0QHU25SEAw&usg=AFQjCNFbTjdBOVaTgllyr63tRcC
mOBdgNw&sig2=LcNX3VuwcsQA2HzuUW49Pw

Kozol, J. (1991). *Savage inequalities: Children in America's schools.* New York: Crown.

Lohr, S. (2009, August 19). Study finds that online education beats the classroom. *New York Times.* bits.blogs.nytimes.com/2009/08/19/study-finds-that-online-education-beats-the-classroom/

Marzano, R. J. (2006). *Classroom assessment & grading that work.* Alexandria, VA: Association for Supervision & Curriculum Development.

McLaughlin, R. (2010, May). *Opening remarks.* New Hampshire Summit on Developing 21st Century Educators. Southern New Hampshire University, Manchester, NH.

Medina, J. (2009). *Brain rules: 12 principles for surviving and thriving at work, home, and school.* Seattle, WA: Pear Press.

New England Secondary School Consortium. (2010). *Dropouts and completers.* Education.nh.gov/data/dropouts.htm

New Hampshire Department of Education. (2007). *New Hampshire's vision for redesign: Moving from high schools to learning communities.* Concord, NH: Author.

New Hampshire Department of Education. (2010, May 26). *New Hampshire Summit on redefining educator development for 21st century learners.* Southern New Hampshire University, Manchester, NH.

New Hampshire Department of Education. (2012). *New Hampshire Annual Dropout Rate.* Concord, NH: Author. Retrieved February 7, 2012, from http://www.education.nh.gov/data/documents/dropout10-11.pdf

Oberlies, K. (2011). *Extended learning opportunities.* Speech delivered at New Hampshire Department of Education, Concord, NH. http://www.education.nh.gov/spotlight/elos.htm

O'Connor, K. (2009). *How to grade for learning, K–12.* Thousand Oaks, CA: Corwin.

Pew Research Center. (2010). *The Millennials: Confident, connected, open to change.* Retrieved from http://pewresearch.org/millennials/

Prensky, M. R. (2010). *Teaching digital natives: Partnering for real learning.* Thousand Oaks, CA: Corwin.

Putnam, R. D. (2001). *Bowling alone: The collapse and revival of American community.* New York: Touchstone.

Quaglia Institute for Student Aspirations. (2009). *My Voice survey: Qualitatively assessing the impact in New Hampshire.* Portland, ME: Author. https://docs.google.com/viewer?a=v&q=cache:ABw5Sp7VTqIJ:www.qisa.org/publications/docs/MyVoice-QualitativeSummaryNH.pdf+&hl=en&gl=us&pid=bl&srcid=ADGEESjDMvONh6DM4DHPcKjv3ai0AQx1bb7VlAqe4MqDg6hFoAELFLPASvs2esA7ndRo5zaGZmZqbKZ28uW6CiWX85NKl76NJzFYQUKSCI2MJlfsme7Wd6bWvNl9rymrEke2X0jQtwkI&sig=AHIEtbRfYoFpp6ydtpBmS-x1ObxGyiP_mA&pli=

Relative to the Renomination or Reelection of Teachers and Grievance Procedures, SB 196-Final Version, New Hampshire Legislature, regular session (2011).

Stiggins, R. J., Arter, J. A., Chappuis, J., & Chappuis, S. (2009). *Classroom assessment for student learning: Doing it right—using it well.* Boston: Allyn & Bacon.

Stucker, K. (2010, November 10). New Hampshire's leading way in lowering dropout rate, boosting graduation rate. *Foster's Daily Democrat,* 1.

United States Department of Labor, Bureau of Labor Statistics. (2010, September). *Number of jobs held, labor market activity, and earnings growth among the youngest Baby Boomers: Results from a longitudinal survey.* Washington, DC: U.S. Government Printing Office. www.bls.gov/news.release/pdf/nlsoy.pdf

Wheeler, T. J. (2004). Address at the New Hampshire Music Education Octoberfest. Manchester Community School, Manchester, NH.

Wiggins, G., & McTighe, J. (2005). *Understanding by design, expanded 2nd edition.* Alexandria, VA: Association for Supervision and Curriculum Development.

Wormeli, R. (2006). *Fair isn't always equal.* Portland, ME: Stenhouse.

Index

CORWIN

A SAGE Company

The Corwin logo—a raven striding across an open book—represents the union of courage and learning. Corwin is committed to improving education for all learners by publishing books and other professional development resources for those serving the field of PreK–12 education. By providing practical, hands-on materials, Corwin continues to carry out the promise of its motto: **"Helping Educators Do Their Work Better."**